Yale Studies in Political Science, 18

Published under the direction of the Department of Political Science

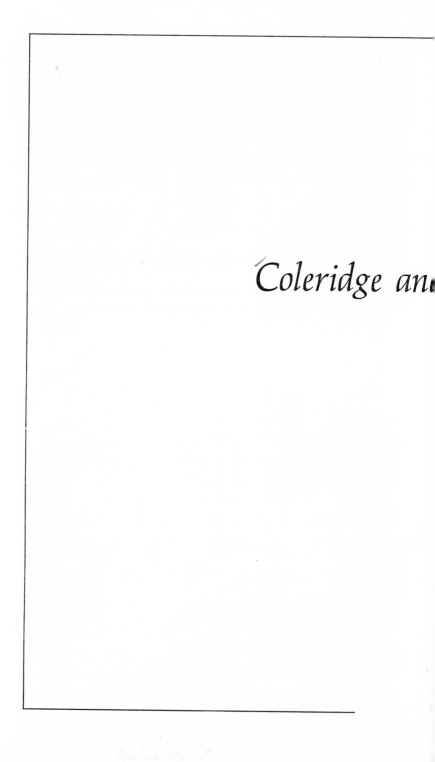

Coleridge an

David P. Calleo

WITHDRAWI

ie Idea of the Modern State

ew Haven and London / Yale University Press / 1966

Library of Congress catalog card number: 66–12488

To Joseph Toy Curtiss

Preface

Anyone who has studied Coleridge knows the difficulties of stalking his protean ideas through his anfractuous prose. Doubtless it is true that his faults are also his virtues. There is no shortage, after all, of modern theories that are admirably systematic—but vacant. Coleridge's writings are a rambling warehouse, badly arranged—but full of treasure. His strength is that he remained a poet after he became a philosopher and seldom allowed the stern demands of a philosopher's system to overrule the poet's insight. He did love too much to play with his thoughts, but the result is that beguiling *wunderlicht* quality that flickers over the swamp.

All these virtuous faults, however, have made the present task especially difficult. For I have tried to present from Coleridge a tolerably complete and coherent theory of the nation-state. My approach has necessarily been different from that of most other Coleridge scholars in that I have been interested in his final systematic views rather than the admittedly fascinating process of their development. I have therefore focused chiefly on what was written or revised after 1815, not because his earlier political writings are uninteresting, but because they represent particular insights and enthusiasms more than reflections of settled views. My formulation will inevitably do violence to some of his random observations, particular stages, and discursive moods. But I presume that Coleridge's thoughts were, as he hoped, a living whole, however rich in perceptive detail, and not "an immense heap of little things"—that the bones of system did develop in his imaginary body-politic. Coleridge is presented in this study as a modern political theorist whose ideas remain potent. The role would not have displeased him. It is as great a compliment as one generation can pay to another.

The book was written in 1963. The last chapter, with its discussion of postwar European federalism, has deliberately been left unchanged, although institutions and views in Europe are, of course, continually changing. The chapter seeks to illustrate an influential modern alternative to Coleridge's way of looking at the nature of a political community, and not to provide an exhaustive analysis of the Common Market today.

This study owes a great deal to others at Yale. Professor Lewis P. Curtis introduced me to Coleridge's writings and their richness. Professors Joseph T. Curtiss and Frederick M. Watkins read the manuscript several times and offered numerous useful suggestions and much kind encouragement. Professors Edzard Baumann, William H. Dunham, E. Donald Hirsch, Jr., George A. Schrader, Jr., and Paul Weiss at one time or another read particular chapters and suggested improvements. They of course are not responsible for any of the mistakes, but they are likely to recognize whatever particular excellences may from time to time appear.

I am grateful to Aldwyne H. B. Coleridge for permission to quote from Coleridge manuscripts and to Kathleen Coburn for her occasional kind assistance and general good will. My study of the Coleridge Notebooks in London owes much to the kindness of Rosemary Davidson.

Much is owed as well to the four undergraduates who acted as critical scribes and diligent researchers: Allan M. Chapin, Anthony O. Edmonds, André F. Houston, and Peter G. Stillman. And finally, there is the debt to my two friends Henry Cooper and Douglas Crowley and those unfortunately anonymous Oxford undergraduates who, on a deceptively placid summer day, rescued the entire manuscript from the Aegean.

D. P. C.

New Haven
April 1965

Contents

INTRODUCTION

Coleridge and the Conservative Ideal

Among all the great literary figures England has produced, Samuel Taylor Coleridge was certainly the most versatile.[1] Three great poems attest to his genius as a poet. He was a newspaper editorialist of unusual merit and considerable popularity. He remains today one of the dominant figures in English literary criticism. Modern students have discovered that he was a great psychologist, a discerning analyst of the creative processes of the human mind. His once-despised philosophy has been carefully studied in recent years, and scholars have been impressed by his accomplishments even in such technical subjects as logic. He was a major figure in the development of modern religious thought in England. He has even been hailed as the forerunner of Keynesian economics!

Yet there have always been scoffers. His contemporaries left some devastatingly unflattering portraits. No man ever had more condescending biographers. He is perennially the weak-willed

1. Samuel Taylor Coleridge (1772–1834) was born in Ottery St. Mary, Devonshire. His father, the Reverend John Coleridge, was the local rector and master of the local grammar school. Samuel Taylor was the youngest of several children. He was sent to Christ's Hospital and in February 1791 was entered at Jesus College, Cambridge. He left without a degree. The next few years were occupied with various literary and political endeavors —including the famous *Pantisocracy*. In 1795 he married Sarah Fricker and commenced his long and highly productive friendship with Wordsworth. The years of his early manhood were the period of his greatest poetic creativity. He was also a successful political editorialist for the *Morning Post*. In 1798, with William and Dorothy Wordsworth, Coleridge visited Germany and was greatly stimulated by its general philosophical

1

genius who pickled his mind in tears of self-pity and dissipated his many talents in abandoned garrulity. His private life was a scandal. He deserted, or rather retreated from, his wife and children. He was a drug addict. Furthermore, he has been found to have appropriated silently far more than was respectable from his German models.

Coleridge's admirers have answers to charges of this kind. What is more damaging to his reputation is the unfinished state of many of his writings. Coleridge often talked as if he hoped to write a grand philosophical synthesis that would tie together his many insights. He never did. Coleridge was not a Romantic Aquinas, an English Hegel. He left behind a heap of glittering fragments—parts of great works that were forever being discussed, but never finished.

He did, however, publish a great deal. And throughout his writings, finished and unfinished, he exhibited not only vast knowledge but a powerful synthesizing imagination, a genius for perceiving the subtle but vital relationships between ideas in one field and those in another. In making a point, he was likely to wander from politics through philosophy, religion, science, and art. Generally the unsympathetic reader is soon lost and transfers his confusion to the author. But Coleridge is a writer who repays careful and persistent study. And however noisy his detractors have been, there has remained from the beginning a devoted band of admirers. Perhaps the most generous tribute ever given to Coleridge came from John Stuart Mill, hardly a disciple:

> There are two men, recently deceased, to whom their country is indebted not only for the greater part of the im-

climate. He visited the Mediterranean from 1804 to 1806, and for ten months acted as secretary to the governor of Malta. In later years his attention turned increasingly toward criticism and philosophy, and he published numerous prose works. He also achieved considerable success as a lecturer and wrote a play that was moderately successful. His attempt to cure himself of opium addiction led him, in 1816, to take up residence in the home of his friend Dr. James Gillman, in Highgate. For the rest of his life, Coleridge hardly ever left Highgate, although he was frequently visited by an increasing number of admirers and disciples, especially among the young. His unhappy marriage produced three children who survived infancy—Hartley, Berkeley, and Sara—all of whom attained some prominence in English intellectual life.

portant ideas which have been thrown into circulation among its thinking men in their time, but for a revolution in its general modes of thought and investigation . . . there is hardly to be found in England an individual of any importance in the world of mind, who (whatever opinions he may have afterwards adopted) did not first learn to think from one of these two . . . These men are, Jeremy Bentham and Samuel Taylor Coleridge—the two great seminal minds of England in their age.[2]

Coleridge was a great seminal mind of the age not as a poet, but as a philosopher. A portion of his philosophy that has not only been influential, but is perhaps the most complete and coherent, is his political theory. Coleridge is sometimes lumped together with his contemporaries Wordsworth and Southey as one of those poets who began as Revolutionaries, grew older and sadder, and ended as Tories. Superficially that was the pattern. He began as a Unitarian preacher, scornful of the Establishment. He was thrilled

When France in wrath her giant-limbs upreared,
And with that oath, which smote air, earth, and sea,
Stamped her strong foot and said she would be free . . .

He loathed aristocrats. He was a disciple of Hartley and fervently believed that men would be good if only their surroundings were improved. He and his friends tried to found an ideal community in America—"Pantisocracy."

But by the time Coleridge came to die in 1834 he was an opponent of Whig reform and a militant champion of Church Establishment. Why? It is easy enough to find apparent causes— French excesses, his own bad health, unhappiness, failing poetical powers, or plain old age. These explanations overlook the fact that Coleridge's later political philosophy is not a melancholy record of declining energy, but an important moment in the creation of a dynamic conservative tradition in English political thought. For it is Coleridge even more than Burke who is the true philosopher of that tradition.

2. John Stuart Mill, "Bentham", *Dissertations and Discussions* (2 vols. London, 1859), *1*, 330–31. (First published in *London and Westminster Review*, August 1838).

To call Coleridge a conservative at all can easily be misleading, especially if conservatism is seen simply as antagonism to change. Coleridge's variety of conservatism defies simple classification. It is not immediately tied to the interests of any one class—although it does, perhaps, point to an alliance of the aristocracy with the lower classes. It is conservatism with a strong radical impulse, for Coleridge was greatly dissatisfied with the status quo. Although he searched the past for principles, he was not merely a political antiquarian. He had no simple-minded desire to reverse history and return to some arbitrarily chosen and sentimentalized moment in the past. Rather he hoped to be able to distill from English history the essential principles which he believed always governed English politics and society in its happier days. These principles must, he thought, serve as guides to present policy. They must be adapted and perhaps compromised, but never neglected. This was a kind of conservatism that could be said to be expedient without being unprincipled. At best, it could not only accept change gracefully, but work imaginatively to perfect the present in the light of old principles.

This capability was sorely needed by conservatives in Coleridge's day. They were quite unprepared for the savage challenge of the French Revolution. The eighteenth century in England had been a prosperous and tranquil era. Compared to the French, the English had taken their Enlightenment rather gracefully. The violent religious controversies of the seventeenth century had subsided. During the eighteenth century, the Established Church maintained a character of good-natured vagueness and for the most part succeeded in avoiding bitter religious divisions. Deism, though at one time widespread among the more intellectual, was considered bad form and was seldom publicly defended. Politically, England enjoyed a rotund complacency that was the envy of Europe. The English revered their Constitution as the nearly miraculous contrivance of the world's wisest people. Throughout much of their eighteenth century, politics turned about personalities and graft—the comfortable indulgences of a prosperous nation free from any seriously divisive issues.

The violent explosion of the Revolution in Paris shocked and frightened many Englishmen. The whole world seemed to be falling to pieces. Who knew where the frenzy would end? Burke

4

soon made everyone aware of the relation between the rationalistic ideas of the French Enlightenment and the political behavior of the Revolutionaries. This knowledge proved nearly fatal to conservative tactics. Terrified by Jacobin principles, the English Tories seemed driven to deny the relevance of any ideals to politics. Burke himself, in condemning the uncritical use of abstract principles to overturn the venerable contrivances of human experience, often seemed to be attacking principle itself. It was easy for men of less vision and virtue to translate hatred for Jacobin rationalism into a disregard for rational principles of any kind. And, what was especially sinister, such an attitude often led to a near hysterical reliance upon repressive force as the sole means for combating hostile ideology.

Coleridge was wise enough to see that it would never be possible to defeat Jacobinism by anti-Jacobinism alone. The very strength of the Revolution was its appeal to humanity and intellect—to the nobler qualities of all men. If its appeal was a false one, Coleridge argued, it could not be countered by attacking altruism and reason, but rather by proposing to men's minds and hearts true political ideals. Coleridge was far from unaware of the heady effects of Revolutionary idealism upon those of generous and ardent character. After all, the young Coleridge had been a hot and radical youth, stirred by the great events of the times and deeply affected by the general enthusiasm for reform. And although he soon repudiated the course the Revolution had taken, he never gave up the habit of looking for a better world. He remained at heart the young Romantic visionary. His whole spirit rejected the cold polish and cynical indifference of the *ancien régime*. He came to defend and admire aristocracy, but his aristocrat was young Harry Coningsby, not Lord Monmouth.[3] Coleridge had always admired Burke, but never the younger Pitt. He never could accept the kind of pragmatic conservatism that eschews idealism altogether. It is this that makes him so distinctive among conservatives. Like so many of his generation, he learned from the bloody failure of the Revolution about sin, about the inevitable limits of human endeavor. But he remained an idealist, convinced of the need for a positive political faith. It

3. See Benjamin Disraeli's novel, *Coningsby* (London, 1844).

was not idealism that was at fault in the Revolution, he argued, but rather the simple-minded ideals of the French. What was needed to combat these false ideals was not selfish cynicism, but alternative ideals more properly suited to the realities of human nature.

Coleridge devoted much of his life to the development of these ideas. He sought to spell out the nature of the good society and the principles and habits that must guide it through history. He built up a theory of the ideal constitutional state in which he sought to reconcile traditional humanism and constitutionalism with the conditions of his time. The result is a wonderfully suggestive theory of the modern national State. It is a vision, an ideal that has haunted English political thought ever since. It has inspired numerous movements, some sound and some foolish. But in the end it seems that the conservatives have received the greatest benefits. For the ideal Coleridge did so much to develop and set loose gave to the conservative principles and goals of his own. No longer was he necessarily tied as a reluctant captive to the liberal chariot.

In nineteenth-century England, the capacity of the traditional order to give way and yet persist was extraordinary. Although industrialization was further advanced in England than anywhere else, England was the only principal Western nation to avoid a major revolution. While the United States fought the Civil War and France sought refuge from revolution in its second Napoleonic dictator, England basked in the Victorian Compromise. Obviously, there were numerous causes for this relatively peaceful adaptation, but important among them was the character of the conservative response to change. English conservatism has frequently been admired, but perhaps for the wrong reasons. Its great achievement was not merely that it knew when to give way gracefully to radical pressure. To be sure, the English did manage to reconcile what Coleridge called "Permanence" and "Progression." They achieved more, however, than a reconciliation. They achieved a genuine synthesis.

Obviously the old order was driven to react only because of insistent radical pressure. That is not surprising. It happened everywhere. What was unique in England was the creativity of the conservative response. The imaginative behavior of conservative statesmen was not altogether unself-conscious. They were informed by a conservative idealism which, while it was present in Burke, found its most complete and systematic expression in Coleridge. Coleridge was remarkable not because he understood the past, but because he pointed so clearly to the future. The constitutional democratic nation-states of the Western world today are far closer to the ideal spelled out by Coleridge than to the visions of his Revolutionary opponents. It was Coleridge, rather than Paine or Bentham, who understood what the moral foundation of the modern State was to be.[4] It was the conservatives, Burke and Coleridge, who saw most clearly into the future.

Nowadays Coleridge is little known as a political theorist. Indeed, surprisingly little is known about English conservative thought. Perhaps that is as it should be. Ideas may sometimes, like men, grow too old for the times. The principles of one age and place may not be pertinent for another. Perhaps, as is often suggested, the national State has itself become a bankrupt idea. Hence those writers who sought so earnestly to comprehend its foundations are irrelevant to the problems of the contemporary world. I do not share this view.

In this book, I shall attempt to set forth Coleridge's whole view of the State and the assumptions upon which his theories rested. I shall not try to assess his influence on later thinkers and politicians. Coleridge was one of those thinkers who was "in the air." To do a proper study of his influence would require an extensive survey of modern English political thought.[5] Furthermore,

---

4. This assertion can certainly be reasonably contested, at least in respect to Bentham. No one can deny that Bentham and his followers made enormous contributions to the theory and practice of government administration in England and in that sense were far more modern than Coleridge. But Bentham's philosophical grasp of the nature of a political community and the forces that maintain it was relatively primitive. His political ideas and those of Paine may have been extraordinarily potent ideological weapons in bringing about admirable reforms, but as comprehensive analyses of the nation-state, either as it was or was going to be, they are deficient. No doubt the chief weakness of Bentham as a political philosopher stemmed from his pleasure–pain psychology.

5. For a discussion of Coleridge's influence see the works by Blunden and Griggs, Boulger, Cobban, Colmer, Kennedy, Mill, and Muirhead listed in the bibliography.

I am not as interested here in what others took from Coleridge as in what he himself actually said. I do believe, on the other hand, that there is much in Coleridge that can profitably be studied in our time and country. For this reason I shall attempt more than an exposition of his ideas, and will suggest, in conclusion, the present relevance of his whole way of looking at the State. Projecting the ideas of the past to the present is always hazardous, but no one can deny that the attempt is Coleridgean in spirit, if not in quality. In our age, as in his own, Coleridge may offer some assistance to those who are seeking an escape from the reigning clichés of contemporary politics.

CHAPTER 1

Leadership and Vision

Throughout his entire life, Coleridge was profoundly dissatisfied with the condition of England. That in itself was not particularly exceptional. So were many others in his day. Coleridge, however, was not only unhappy with the status quo, but as his thinking developed he opposed nearly all contemporary movements for reform.

Much as he criticized the established Church of England, he came to prefer it to evangelical or nonconformist alternatives. While he had little liking for Pitt and his Tories, he grew to despise the home-grown Revolutionaries—the Paines, Prices, and Cartwrights. The great Utilitarian crusade for reform, led by men like Bentham and James Mill, was based upon principles repugnant to Coleridge. For him these "Neo-Epicureans" were the quintessence of all the malignant influences poisoning English life.

The besetting sin of radicals and reactionaries alike, Coleridge believed, was their fatal love for abstraction and oversimplification. Their theories were all "partial" views, based upon too narrow a notion of man and human society. Hence they had no real understanding of politics or economics. Their remedies were seldom effective and often harmful. Coleridge's first major political works, *The Friend* and the *Lay Sermons*, contained exhaustive critiques of such partial views. He singled out in particular the democratic Utopians, the Tory reactionaries, and the English political economists. The next several chapters are devoted to an examination of these critiques, beginning with the political economists.

9

Coleridge's writings are filled with attacks on the great tradition of Smith, Malthus, Ricardo, and Bentham. The most thorough and systematic critique came in 1817 with the publication of the second *Lay Sermon*—an analysis of the existing distresses and discontents of English society. The discontents were considerable. The period was one of astonishing vitality and change. The economic revolution that had been taking place in England for many decades was given tremendous impetus by the Napoleonic Wars. By 1815 England was on the threshold of the modern industrial world. However impressive the achievements, the problems to be solved were formidable even by our present standards of crisis: sharp business fluctuations, an enormous national debt, disruption of agriculture, rapid growth and urbanization of the population, misery and degradation among the lower classes, decline of traditional beliefs, institutions, and allegiances, and corresponding restlessness among the newly rich and the newly poor. Exacerbating all these difficulties was the memory of the French Revolution itself, combining lofty idealism, incendiary demagoguery, and an unprecedented mobilization of national power and enthusiasm.

The political economists had become the ideological champions of the new middle class and the commercial society it was creating. The whole school had become dominated by the belief that scarcity was the most significant and permanent characteristic of human life. Man's world was harsh. Only the most constant and arduous exertion would produce enough to maintain civilized society. There might be progress for a time and even an unnatural plenty. But ultimately the gloomy laws of the dismal science of economics would reassert their force. Malthus sadly observed that productive capacity was inherently incapable of keeping pace with population.

Ricardo gave a classical formulation to the economic dilemma: "The natural price of labour is that price which is necessary to enable the labourers, one with another, to subsist and to perpetuate their race, without either increase or diminution."[1] In a potentially wealthy but undercapitalized and perhaps underpopu-

1. David Ricardo, "On the Principles of Political Economy and Taxation," *Works of David Ricardo*, ed. Piero Sraffa (10 vols. Cambridge, England, 1951–55), *1*, 93.

lated country, initial increases in capital may have great effect on production and may even lead to large surpluses that will result in still more capital. But as the population inexorably increases, production will inevitably lag behind. More and more will be needed for consumption. As the economy becomes increasingly capitalized, new capital will lose its magical ability to cause dramatic expansions of production:

> Although, then, it is probable, that under the most favourable circumstances, the power of production is still greater than that of population, it will not long continue so; for the land being limited in quantity, and differing in quality, with every increased portion of capital employed on it, there will be a decreased rate of production, whilst the power of population continues always the same.[2]

The "Iron Law of Wages" will reassert itself and the earnings of the laborers will fall to their "natural" level, or worse. Yet any attempt to tamper with these disagreeable regulators of economic life will only worsen the situation. Relief financed by taxes will eventually decrease production:

> There are no taxes which have not a tendency to lessen the power to accumulate. . . . Some taxes will produce these effects in a much greater degree than others: but the great evil of taxation is to be found, not so much in any selection of its objects, as in the general amount of its effects taken collectively.[3]

Despoiling the rich will only increase the misery of the poor. Since capital comes from surplus, any reduction of profits will eventually reduce the formation of capital. Production will then fall even further behind population until privation, pestilence, or self-regulation have righted the balance.

For this whole system, Coleridge entertained the most indignant contempt. Political economy was to him a science that began with a view of man that was patently an abstraction designed to exclude all those human characteristics not subject to technical

2. Ibid., p. 98.
3. Ibid., p. 152.

11

calculation. The political economists' view of society was even more abstract:

> They worship a kind of nonentity under the different words, the state, the whole, the society, and so on, and to this idol they make bloodier sacrifices than ever the Mexicans did to Tescalipoca.[4]

> the nearest approach to the realization of such a state is a colony, composed of a 100 wealthy Planters, and a 100,000 Slaves, the surplus value of whose labor above the price of their scanty food and cloathing centers in the 100.[5]

In their manic preoccupation with production, Coleridge believed, the economists ignored every other value by which man lives:

> the remainder of the population mechanized into engines for the manufactory of new rich men;—yea, the machinery of the wealth of the nation made up of the wretchedness, disease, and depravity of those who should constitute the strength of the nation! Disease, I say, and vice, while the wheels are in full motion; but at the first stop the magic wealth-machine is converted into an intolerable weight of pauperism.[6]

What if these methods had succeeded in their object and there had been in fact an enormous increase in production? Coleridge asked but one question:

> Has the national welfare, have the weal and happiness of the people, advanced with the increase of the circumstantial prosperity? Is the increasing number of wealthy individuals that which ought to be understood by the wealth of the nation?[7]

He answered his own question with an emphatic "No!"

4. Samuel Taylor Coleridge, "The Friend," *The Complete Works of Samuel Taylor Coleridge*, ed. W. G. T. Shedd (7 vols. New York, 1858–68), 2, 272.

5. *Memoranda suggested during a Perusal of the Minutes of Evidence before the Select Committee on the State of Children employed in Manufacture*, 1816 (Berg Collection, New York Public Library).

6. Coleridge, "Church and State," *Works*, 6, 64.

7. Ibid.

Coleridge was among the first in England to challenge the materialism of the reigning economic school and to demand that economic "science" take account of the needs of the whole man and the whole society. In effect he argued that the health of the nation could no more be measured by commercial prosperity alone than the health of a man could be measured by the size of his waistline. The true health of England had been sadly jeopardized in his opinion by the economist's predilection for seeing all things solely through the "medium of the market."

Coleridge's fundamental approach to economic questions is well illustrated in his discussion of the disciplinary role of the laws of supply and demand working through the business cycle, the salutary means by which, in classical economics, excess growth is pruned and production readjusted to normal supply and demand. Doubtless business does find its own level, Coleridge observed, but what of the hapless and often innocent individuals crushed in the process:

> But persons are not things—but man does not find his level. Neither in body nor in soul does the man find his level. After a hard and calamitous season, during which the thousand wheels of some vast manufactory had remained silent as a frozen waterfall, be it that plenty has returned and that trade has once more become brisk and stirring: go, ask the overseer, and question the parish doctor, whether the workman's health and temperance with the staid and respectful manners best taught by the inward dignity of conscious self-support, have found their level again! Alas! I have more than once seen a group of children in Dorsetshire, during the heat of the dog-days, each with its little shoulders up to its ears, and its chest pinched inward, the very habit and fixtures, as it were, that had been impressed on their frames by the former ill-fed, ill-clothed, and unfuelled winters.[8]

The natural workings of the business cycle bring not only hardship to the poor, but moral decay to the rest of society:

8. Coleridge, "Lay Sermon," *Works*, 6, 209.

But as with the body, so or still worse with the mind. Nor is the effect confined to the laboring classes, whom by an ominous but too appropriate change in our phraseology we are now accustomed to call the laboring poor. I cannot persuade myself that the frequency of failures with all the disgraceful secrets of fraud and folly, of unprincipled vanity in expending and desperate speculation in retrieving, can be familiarized to the thoughts and experience of men, as matters of daily occurrence, without serious injury to the moral sense.[9]

Coleridge's attitude toward economic processes was surprisingly modern. He was among the first to grasp the possibly beneficial effects of taxation and national debt and to have some comprehension of the role of credit. Taxes, in his view, need not impoverish the nation. They redistribute rather than deplete!

It is demonstrable that taxes, the product of which is circulated in the country from which they are raised, can never injure a country directly by the mere amount; but either from the time or circumstances under which they are raised, or from the injudicious mode in which they are levied, or from the improper objects to which they are applied.[10]

Like the sun, taxes may take moisture from the swamp and rain it down upon the plain, or, conversely, from the plain to the swamp.

In fact, Coleridge argued, the tremendous increase in government expenditures during the Napoleonic Wars, far from ruining England, caused unparalleled prosperity and expansion. The ensuing depression was the result of an over-sudden return to "sound" fiscal policy. Because of the clamor of the economists against taxation, postwar "Retrenchment could no longer proceed by cautious and calculated steps; but was compelled to hurry forward, like one who crossing the sands at too late an hour finds himself threatened by the inrush of the tide."[11] The

9. Ibid.
10. Ibid., p. 172.
11. Ibid., p. 175.

"vulgar" errors of the economists served only to exacerbate the evil effects of a painful readjustment.

Coleridge's significance to economic thought is derived, however, not from his random anticipations of modern techniques of economic planning, but from his early attack upon the classical notion that the chief concern of economics is production rather than distribution. For Coleridge, economics does not properly dictate social values; it serves them. In order to adopt this view, he had to deny the fundamental assumption of the political economists that human society is doomed to natural scarcity. In the *Lay Sermon* he observed:

> I have, at least, met with no proof that there is or has been any scarcity, either in the materials of all necessary comforts, or any lack of strength, skill, and industry to prepare them.[12]

If the society of the day was not sufficiently affluent to satisfy all the demands upon it, the cause lay in inflated demands rather than in a short supply. The English economy was compared to "a man in health pining at a full table because there was not *the savoury meat there which he loved.*" If he were starving, the cause was not natural scarcity, but "the man's own undisciplined temper, or habits of self-indulgence."[13] In short, there was ample wealth in England—enough to keep both rich and poor in the comforts reasonable for their station. There was no natural scarcity that condemned the poor to ceaseless and wretched toil. Such scarcity could only be induced by the unnatural and insatiable greed of men who sacrificed all other values for the pursuit of material gain. Coleridge observed that the "Spirit of Commerce" had run wild, trampling over patriotism, religion, learning, humanity itself. Economic gain had become the only standard of value. Nothing was immune from the habit of looking "at all things through the *medium* of the market."[14] Whatever the short-term causes of distress, it was rampant commercialism that was the fundamental cause for the profound disquiet and instability in English society.

12. Ibid., p. 181.
13. Ibid.
14. Ibid., p. 196.

Coleridge's analysis differed from that of the political economists in two important respects. He focused on demand rather than supply, and his economic analysis placed great stress on the importance of cultural factors. For him production was not necessarily a more pressing consideration than distribution. Scarcity was not the inevitable condition of modern economies.

In his opinion the British economy was in fact sufficiently affluent to meet the legitimate demands upon it. The problem was not with supply, but with demand—the excessive demand of the holders of capital. It was this that led to the unfortunate pattern of distribution. Why was this demand met at such expense to the rest of society? Not for any purely economic reason, Coleridge argued. For in an abundant economy the pattern of distribution is not predetermined by the physical needs of man, but is determined in large part by the cultural values of the society. Thus the current ills of England were essentially cultural in origin. The very commercialism that had led to the startling growth of production had caused an inflated demand for capital and the resultant scarcity that condemned a large segment of the population to hopeless and wretched toil. The rich had been taking a disproportionate share of the new wealth at great cost to the character of the nation.

The accuracy of Coleridge's analysis of the British economy is, of course, highly debatable.[15] What is significant here, however, is the relationship between his economic views and his gen-

15. A well-known group of contemporary economists and economic historians has of course asserted that the relative misery of factory workers in the early nineteenth century was and is a myth, exploited first by the conservatives and later by Marx, Engels, and the socialists, but not supported by a close examination of the facts. It was industrialization, the rise in productivity, which brought about the enormous rise in the standard of living for a greatly increased working population. See for example the essays by F. A. Hayek and T. S. Ashton in F. A. Hayek, ed., *Capitalism and the Historians* (Chicago, 1954). It should be noted incidentally that Coleridge did not deny that industrialization had resulted in a great increase in productivity which had benefited the workers. What he did object to was the cyclical nature of industrial economy and the assumption that its effects are beneficial to society. It should also be noted that the *Lay Sermon* was published in 1817, during a period when the condition of the worker was, Ashton admits, exceptionally depressed. See *Capitalism and the Historians*, p. 135.

eral political theory. Since he believed that demand and distribution were functions of the cultural values of society, he naturally concluded that an economic theory that did not take account of moral, cultural, and psychological factors was unlikely either to understand or cure the current ills of England. Indeed, he argued, the political economists, with their absurdly limited view of man and society, only made the situation worse. With their erroneous emphasis on scarcity they provided a "scientific" excuse for rapaciousness. Political economy was the ideology of greed. It was itself an illustration of the cultural illness that had made commercial values so dominant.

Coleridge was sensible enough not to try to build an economic theory out of an attack on human greed. He was cured of Pantisocracy. Greed and competition were facts of life. There was nothing wrong in itself with the "Spirit of Commerce." Indeed, commercialism had been the chief spur, not only to material progress, but to political liberty as well. But, he argued, commercial values must not be extended beyond their proper sphere. Economic wealth and efficiency are not the sole standards for the general welfare. Man is more than a hungry animal and the State is more than an aggregate of consumers. The trouble in England came not from the tremendous increase in economic energy, which itself was good. The trouble came from the weakness of those elements of national life that were meant to counterbalance commercialism. They had not merely failed to keep pace with economic growth; they had actually declined. As a result of the general weakness of the culture, economic growth was a curse rather than a blessing.

Coleridge specified three cultural attitudes that had traditionally balanced commercial values: deference to the aristocracy and its code, religious feeling, and passion and respect for true philosophical and scientific learning. The first check was undermined as the aristocracy itself was invaded by the newly rich. Coleridge admitted that the former unattainable eminence of the great families was not without several abuses; "still, this reverence for ancientry in families acted as a counterpoise to the grosser superstition of wealth."[16] The reverence diminished as titles became more accessible.

16. Coleridge, "Lay Sermon," *Works*, 6, 183.

Meanwhile the second check, religion, had abandoned its spiritual dimension and was reduced to a series of prudential maxims to insure commercial reliability. Coleridge despaired of the state of theological knowledge and interest among the clergy themselves. The Church of England seemed established upon:

> that cowardly half-in-half semi-moral, semi-theological, only wholly unspiritual, fluctuating yet most intolerant, *tacit Compact* of Belief, the *tone* of which is given by the preferment-hunting Party of *discreet correct* Dignitaries and Expectants of Dignities—men with whom a doubt as to the authenticity of Daniel and even of the six first Chapters would damn a Clergyman far more than a disbelief of every one of the spiritual Ideas that constitute Christianity.[17]

> It is not the necessity of believing the 39 Articles; which not one in a thousand professes (to his own mind) to believe— but among many, perhaps, a majority the impression . . . that if they were to examine the subject as they would any other subject, they should disbelieve them—and therefore get rid of the risk by not studying theology at all.[18]

Coleridge was even more critical of the evangelical and dissenting Christians. They took pride in the practicality of their religion. They tended to emphasize piety and good works and were proud that they wasted little time in sterile doctrinal squabbles. As Coleridge saw it, their lack of interest in theology conveniently removed from their religion those intellectual aspects that might take a man's mind off his business. In Coleridge's opinion, few Low Church merchants stood in need of such protection. Their enthusiasm for anything other than business was not likely to get out of control.

Commercialism, Coleridge argued, had swamped not only aristocracy and religion, but science and philosophy as well. The result was that scientist and philosopher had become estranged from each other, and both had descended into shallow materialism. Scientists, in Coleridge's view, were now engaged in an end-

17. Coleridge, Notebook 35, fol. 22ʳ (British Museum Add. MS 47530). Hereinafter cited by Notebook and folio.
18. Notebook 35, fol. 21ᵛ.

less collection of facts without any interest in the deeper insights that give coherence to facts and enable man to comprehend the framework of the physical universe. Indeed, society did its best to lure the scientist from pure research and speculation into the greedy scramble for profitable technological innovation. Coleridge was similarly in despair over the state of contemporary English philosophy. Philosophy supposedly furnishes men with ideals that point to the fuller and richer development of human life. But those whom Coleridge saw as the typical philosophers of the new age—Ricardo, Bentham, and their French sources (the "Neo-Epicureans" as Coleridge called them)—preached a naïve materialism and took an absurdly narrow view of man.

Was it possible that English culture had so declined that someone as preposterous as Bentham could be taken seriously? Bentham, who actually taught that pushpin is as good as poetry and was prepared to build his philosophy upon such an axiom! Coleridge noted in exasperation: "A long and attentive observation had convinced me that formerly men were worse than their principles, but that at present the principles are worse than the men."[19]

To Coleridge the age seemed desperately superficial. How else could men be so easily seduced by such flagrantly partial explanations of politics and life? It was an age of bustling talents, but no genius: "a swarm of clever, well-informed men: an anarchy of minds, a despotism of maxims."[20] As further cause and consequence: the rapid decline of education. No age was more concerned with the spread of learning, or knew less about its real content. Popularization of learning meant "plebification." Gone was the coherence of education. The modern universities presented a scene of industrious anarchy. They were "lecture bazaars." Inevitably there would be a decline in leadership: "Government by clubs of journeymen; by saint and sinner societies, committees, institutions; by reviews, magazines, and, above all, by newspapers."[21] Meanwhile, the steady demoralization of the lower classes: "Gin consumed by paupers to the value of about

---

19. Coleridge, "Lay Sermon," *Works*, 6, 150.
20. Coleridge, "Church and State," *Works*, 6, 66.
21. Ibid.

eighteen millions yearly . . . crimes quadrupled for the whole country, and in some countries decupled."[22]

Heartbreaking cultural decline, springing indirectly from the same cause: the tremendous burgeoning of the commercial spirit and the concurrent decline of its normal counterweights. Hence arose that insatiable lust for material wealth which, in addition to all its other undesirable effects, itself promoted economic instability. What did Coleridge think could be done to restore the balance? He concluded that the "Spirit of Commerce" could be contained by invoking as a counterweight the "Spirit of the State." The invocation makes Coleridge sound more modern than in fact he was, for although his general principles impelled him toward "planning," he was nevertheless skeptical about the ability of government to intervene effectively and chary of anything that might reduce individual rights and responsibilities. It cannot be said too often that by State Coleridge did not mean government. He was not an early Fabian calling for government direction of the economy in the interests of broad social values. He was not even an early Keynesian—although Keynes was clearly influenced by Coleridge's criticism of the Classical School.[23]

Coleridge was nevertheless far less timid about using government to shape the society than contemporary or later devotees of laissez faire. His complacent view of taxes suggests an openminded, undogmatic approach to the use of governmental power and initiative. Government, he held, should be concerned with far more than the essentially negative tasks of protecting the life, personal freedom, property, reputation, and religion of its subjects from foreign or domestic attacks. Indeed, he would assign it some rather far-reaching, if vague, responsibilities for the welfare of each citizen:

> 1, to make the means of subsistence more easy to each individual:—2, to secure to each of its members the hope of bettering his own condition or that of his children:—3, the

22. Ibid., p. 64.

23. For a discussion of Coleridge's influence upon modern economics, see William F. Kennedy, *Humanist versus Economist*, University of California Publications in Economics, 17 (Berkeley, 1958).

development of those faculties which are essential to his humanity, that is, to his rational and moral being.[24]

There were some instances where Coleridge urged the direct intervention of Parliament to improve working conditions—especially for children.[25] But all in all, Coleridge placed little faith in the ability of legislators or bureaucrats to reform society. In his opinion direct government action had too many shortcomings and too many dangers. He had little faith in reform by acts of Parliament: "It is not in the power of a minister or of a cabinet to say to the current of national tendency, Stay here! or, Flow there! The excess can only be remedied by the slow progress of intellect, the influences of religion, and irresistible events guided by Providence."[26] Ultimately, it is not particular legislation, but the general state of public opinion, that determines the character of the society:

> It is no uncommon weakness with those who are honored with the acquaintance of the great, to attribute national events to particular persons, particular measures, to the errors of one man, to the intrigues of another, to any possible spark of a particular occasion, rather than to the true proximate cause (and which alone deserves the name of a cause), the predominant state of public opinion.[27]

Coleridge believed that public opinion is dominated in the long run by what he called "Ideas," notions that are often only dimly comprehended by the average man, but that nevertheless mold his thoughts and perceptions. These dominating Ideas are ultimately derived from the speculations of those few in society who

24. Coleridge, "Church and State," *Works, 6,* 216.

25. See Coleridge, *Memoranda suggested during a Perusal of the Minutes of Evidence before the Select Committee on the State of Children employed in Manufacture,* 1816 (Berg Collection, New York Public Library); and the two pamphlets "Remarks on the Objections which have been urged against the Principle of Sir Robert Peel's Bill" (1818) and "The Grounds of Sir Robert Peel's Bill Vindicated by S. T. Coleridge" (1818), reprinted in *Inquiring Spirit,* ed. Kathleen Coburn (London, 1951).

26. Coleridge, "Lay Sermon," *Works, 6,* 182 n.

27. Coleridge, "The Stateman's Manual," *Works, 1,* 427.

concern themselves with philosophic truth. The great changes in life since Elizabeth's reign:

> had their origin not in the cabinets of statesmen, or in the practical insight of men of business, but in the visions of recluse genius. To the immense majority of men, even in civilized countries, speculative philosophy has ever been, and must ever remain, a *terra incognita*. Yet it is not the less true, that all the epoch-forming revolutions of the Christian world, the revolutions of religion and with them the civil, social, and domestic habits of the nations concerned, have coincided with the rise and fall of metaphysical systems.[28]

Nevertheless, Coleridge argued, reform cannot be imposed by the manipulations of the few until the popularization of ideas has prepared the many. Reformers must always be careful to avoid the error of Milton and his great compatriots. They "were too much Republicans because they were too little Democrats."[29] They sought "changes and beneficent Innovations effected by the *Few*"[30] and committed the error of "aiming at forms of government and institutions beyond the moral and intellectual growth of the Nation at large."[31] Truly effective reform must deal with the public mind. The basic troubles of English society spring from a distortion of values. Balance cannot be restored by government decree, but only through the slow workings of education, philosophy, and religion.

Big government is likely to be not only ineffective, but dangerous. Coleridge, like Burke, and no doubt for the same reasons, saw much to be feared from the penchant for busy legislative meddling. Too many zealous reformers had shown themselves eager to undertake the renovation of society from top to bottom. There was no shortage of these madmen who "dream of digging or blowing up the foundation of a house in order to employ the materials in repairing the walls."[32] The French had learned that

---

28. Ibid., p. 428.
29. Notebook 26, fol. 42ʳ.
30. Notebook 26, fol. 42ᵛ.
31. Ibid.
32. Coleridge, "Lay Sermon," *Works*, 6, 217.

the cure could be worse than the disease. Englishmen of Coleridge's stamp were reluctant to share their experiences.

But if by the "Spirit of the State" Coleridge did not mean government, what did he mean? His definition of "State," so central to his political theory, will be closely analyzed in subsequent chapters. Essentially, however, his State is Burke's moral partnership of men in search of a good life for themselves and their descendants. A good life depends upon the development of those capacities that can only be nurtured in freedom. A meddling, ubiquitous, and paternalistic government denies the individual the necessary elbowroom for his development: "In Tuscany, the Grand Dukes have, I . . . believe, most sincerely desired to act as Fathers to their People; but then it is on the condition, that the People shall remain Children."[33]

Ultimately even the most benevolent despotism defeats the ends of the State, for it results in the degradation of the people. They become fit for nothing but Machiavellian tyranny: "A Tyrant is only a monstrous Phantasm up-streaming from the grave and corruption of the huddled corses of the self-murdered Virtue and inner freedom of the People, *i.e.* the Majority of the Citizens of the State."[34]

Thus if the State is to retain its health, all private rights must be assiduously protected. It is especially important, Coleridge believed, that the legitimate rights of private property be carefully preserved. Private property is indispensable not only to political freedom, but to the moral development and independence of the individual, and that is the chief moral justification of property. Coleridge acknowledged other justifications—Locke's labor theory, for example, which asserts that use creates right. Coleridge agreed that man by his labor on an object "has combined with it many parts of his Being—his knowledge, memory, affections, a sense of right, above all."[35] But in his opinion there are sounder apologies for private ownership. The true defense

33. Notebook 45, fol. 1ᵛ.
34. Notebook 29 as reproduced in *Inquiring Spirit*, ed. Kathleen Coburn (London, 1951) p. 321.
35. Notebook 18, fol. 118ʳ.

of property lies in "the necessity of a sphere of free action" for "the possession of responsible free agency."[36] The moral development of the individual requires a sphere which he can call his own and within which he can exercise choice. This is the fundamental justification for all private rights.

On the other hand Coleridge, unlike the Liberal devotees of laissez faire, did not believe that freedom is, by itself, sufficient to insure a good life, either for the individual or for society. In this respect he agreed more with Hobbes than with Locke. The pursuit of private self-interest by each individual leads not to automatic natural harmony, but to the war of all against all. In Coleridge's view, the ardent pursuit of private property in England was leading not to Utopia, but to the general depreciation of national character and to actual physical misery for the preponderance of the population. Thus, while freedom is necessary for a good life and a good society, it is not sufficient. Order and coordination are also necessary. How can they be achieved without governmental direction? Only if the needed direction and restraint arise primarily from social cooperation and self-discipline. A good society will result not from curtailing individual rights, but from emphasizing that if there are to be rights there must also be correlative duties. The private holders of wealth and power, especially, must accept the responsibility of self-regulation in the national interest. In the last analysis, the safeguard for their freedom is their responsibility and their intelligence. Thus it was a fundamental axiom with Coleridge that rights and duties are interdependent. The State places a moral obligation upon the individual to perform certain duties, but the State must in turn respect certain rights "for there can be no Duties (save to God only) without correlative Rights."[37] The State demands the one but must guarantee the other. The individual claims the one and must perform the other.

Within the English tradition, Coleridge believed that the possession of landed property had always been tied to the assumption of civic responsibility. Neither English law nor history justified treating land as purely personal property. In fact, the

36. Notebook 48, fol. 4^r.
37. Ibid.

possession of landed property had always implied the duties of citizenship:

> [It is] . . . declared by the spirit and history of our laws that the possession of a property, not connected with especial duties, a property not fiduciary or official, but arbitrary and unconditional, was in the sight of our forefathers the brand of a Jew and an alien; not the distinction, nor the right, nor the honor, of an English baron or gentleman.[38]

Coleridge developed an elaborate theory explaining the distinction in law between "personal" and landed property. From the beginning, the law had always seen land as a trust managed by the gentry for the benefit of the entire State. The ends of agriculture are ultimately the same as the ends of the State:

> That agriculture requires principles essentially different from those of trade; that a gentleman ought not to regard his estate as a merchant his cargo, or a shopkeeper his stock, —admits of an easy proof from the different tenure of landed property, and from the purposes of agriculture itself, which ultimately are the same as those of the State of which it is the offspring.[39]

Doubtless the special status accorded the landowner reflected something of Coleridge's own preference for country over town —although whatever admiration he may have possessed for the gentry was not unqualified: "A more short-sighted, selfish, and blundering Body of Statesmen never existed, than the present Country Party . . . The overbalance of the Landed Interest in the H. of C. is the true Evil of the Borough System."[40]

At any rate, in the modern industrial world other forms of capital have displaced the supremacy of land, and Coleridge's distinctions are obviously dated. What remains, however, is the doctrine that property is justified by its necessity as the domain of free agency and that the enjoyment of this right creates the corresponding duty that it be exercised for the good of the whole society.

38. Coleridge, "Church and State," *Works*, 6, 50.
39. Coleridge, "Lay Sermon," *Works*, 6, 215.
40. Notebook 28, fol. 50ʳ.

Coleridge's "Spirit of the State" then does not mean government regulation. It means a conscious concern for the general good. He argued that the sorry condition of contemporary England resulted from the failure of the governing classes to shape their actions in accordance with the general good. Their failure was as much intellectual as moral. Not only did they not perform their duty, but they had no clear conception of where it lay. Their ignorance was pandered to by the economists who replaced the whole man with economic man and saw the State as nothing more than an aggregate of consumers and narrow interests.

Effective reform, Coleridge believed, could ultimately come only through education, particularly education of the governing classes. But what kind of education? Coleridge was quite aware that a good education does not result automatically from the absence of unwholesome influences. It was not enough to rail against false science, religion, morality and politics if there was nothing to substitute for these misshapen ideals. If the Spirit of Commerce enthroned by the economists was a preposterously inadequate guide for the good society, what would replace it? What was the Spirit of the State? As we have seen, it was not the institutions of government. It was instead the notion in men's minds of what constitutes a good society. This notion would ideally comprehend all the values relevant to human life. Coleridge believed it was the ultimate task of philosophy to cultivate and reformulate the social ideal so that the changing requirements of the times could be harmonized with the enduring needs of man. In a sense, all that he ever wrote—poetry and prose alike—was an attempt to provide an adequate contemporary expression of the good life and the good society. As a political philosopher he devoted most of his attention to exposing popular but partial concepts of human nature. It was superficial views of man that led in his opinion to such disastrously false views of society as those presented by the political economists, the Jacobins, and the reactionary Tories. His criticism of the first suggests that his quarrel with all of them was philosophical. They had too narrow a view of human nature and society.

What Coleridge sought to develop was not just a particular program for reform but a whole way of looking at politics and the State. This is not to say that he was unconcerned with the

answers to immediate political questions, but rather that his ultimate concern was for the way in which these questions are
framed and the values that should determine the answers.[41] This
is, in effect, to say nothing more than that Coleridge was a political philosopher. It also suggests that it would be well to discuss
his general character as a philosopher before examining further
his specifically political theories.

41. A recent summary of Coleridge's social ideas and practical political
programs as distinct from his more formal political theory is John Colmer,
Coleridge, Critic of Society (Oxford, 1959).

CHAPTER 2

The Philosophical Underpinnings

Until the last few decades, scholarship has not done justice to the philosophical coherence of Coleridge's writing. His thought was not so much dissected as dismembered. There seems to have been a pronounced tendency among earlier students to pick out a single aspect of his thought and treat it in isolation from all the rest. Indeed, the remainder of his work was often not merely ignored but actually disparaged. Perhaps the practice began with those critics and biographers who saw Coleridge as a great poet, sadly ruined by his weak character and the equally unwholesome effects of opium and German metaphysics. Even more knowledgeable students, while speaking admiringly of Coleridge as a critic, psychologist, or political theorist, have felt impelled to deplore some other aspect of his thought —his wretched metaphysics or driveling economics. Coleridge's theory of the State, wrote one commentator, is profound and provocative, except where it is unfortunately cast over by the sickly glow of philosophical moonshine. Coleridge's philosophical studies, especially, have been taken as an irrelevant and possibly embarrassing encumbrance on his otherwise impressive legacy.[1]

Recent scholarship, the editing of the Notebooks, for example, has revealed not only the astonishing range of Coleridge's knowledge and interests, but has gradually brought to light the coherence and integration of his thinking, as he wanders about in art,

1. For a defense of this practice, see I. A. Richards, *Coleridge on Imagination* (Bloomington, Ind., 1960), p. 10.

science, religion, or politics. Coherence is not at first glance compellingly evident in Coleridge's writings. Indeed, on early acquaintance Coleridge's mind seems a fantastic maze—a maze rooted in a bog. The reader begins to wonder where he is and if there is any way out. But what appear aimless paths turn out to be a series of spokes in a great wheel—emanating from a central concern and exhibiting always a similar way of proceeding. The consistency of his approach is so pronounced that it indicates not only that Coleridge possessed a basic philosophical world-view, but that he strove to reflect it in nearly everything he wrote. It is impossible, therefore, to understand Coleridge's political ideas fully without some comprehension of the essential characteristics of his whole philosophical system.[2]

As Coleridge was consciously concerned with relating his views on particular subjects to his views on life in general, it is not surprising to discover him preoccupied with what he called "method"—the process by which the mind gains knowledge and relates its apprehensions systematically to each other. In Coleridge's view, the mind employs method when it contemplates "not things only, or for their own sake alone, but likewise and chiefly the relations of things, either their relations to each other, or to the observer, or to the state and apprehension of the hearers. To enumerate and analyze these relations, with the conditions under which alone they are discoverable, is to teach the science of method."[3]

Coleridge argued that it is the habit of viewing all things in relation, and more specifically of seeing the general in the particular, that marks the educated mind. Characters from Shakespeare were summoned to illustrate the distinction. When Dame Quickly relates to Falstaff the circumstances of his obligations, her speech is devoid of method. It exhibits only memory at free rein, with no organizing principle other than simple chronology:

---

2. An impressive recent attempt to describe the central tenets of Coleridge's view of reality and to sketch out its methodical application to science and its implications for human affairs can be found in Craig W. Miller, "Coleridge's Concept of Nature," *Journal of the History of Ideas*, 25 (1964), 77–96. A number of good studies of Coleridge's general philosophy are listed in the bibliography.

3. Coleridge, "The Friend," *Works*, 2, 411.

FALSTAFF. What is the gross sum that I owe thee?

HOST. Marry, if thou wert an honest man, thyself and the money too. Thou didst swear to me upon a parcel-gilt goblet, sitting in my Dolphin chamber, at the round table, by a sea-coal fire, upon Wednesday in Whitsun week, when the prince broke thy head for liking his father to a singing-man of Windsor; thou didst swear to me then, as I was washing thy wound, to marry me and make me my lady thy wife. Canst thy deny it? Did not goodwife Keech, the butcher's wife, come in then and call me gossip Quickly?—coming in to borrow a mess of vinegar; telling us she had a good dish of prawns; whereby thou didst desire to eat some; whereby I told thee they were ill for a green wound, &c.[4]

Hamlet, on the other hand, is cited as a classic example of an educated and hence generalizing mind. He is "ever disposed to generalize" and "all the digressions and enlargements consist of reflections, truths, and principles of general and permanent interest, either directly expressed or disguised in playful satire."[5] He tells Horatio the circumstances that led him, on his voyage to England, to discover his stepfather's treachery:

HAM. Sir, in my heart there was a kind of fighting
That would not let me sleep: methought, I lay
Worse than the mutines in the bilboes. Rashly,
And praise be rashness for it—Let us know,
Our indiscretion sometimes serve[s] us well,
When our deep plots do fail: and that should teach us,
There's a divinity that shapes our ends,
Rough-hew them how we will.[6]

Methodical generalization occurs in the educated mind because of the presence of a leading thought, a primary concern—in parliamentary terms the "initiative"—that dominates the train of thought and systematically subordinates lesser ideas and arranges all into a coherent whole.

Generalization, Coleridge noted, may itself be carried to excess.

4. Ibid., p. 410.
5. Ibid., p. 412.
6. Ibid., p. 411.

In Hamlet's case it becomes mania and leads to withdrawal. The melancholy prince retreats from the actual world into an ideal world of "wayward meditation." He suffers from a "consequent indisposition to action."[7] The man with so unbalanced a mind loses contact with "the apprehension and sympathies of his hearers."[8] He also loses contact with the reality that method is meant to discover. For reality is not merely a dead arrangement of static universals, subject to an unalterable order. It is constant change, and any systematic method that ignores particulars will never be able to encompass the flux that is part of reality. True method can therefore never be "a mere dead arrangement containing in itself no principle of progression."[9] It must seek to discover the regulative principles that guide progressive transition. True method consequently must exhibit "that just proportion, that union and interpenetration, of the universal and the particular, which must ever pervade all works of decided genius and true science."[10]

Here is summarized the central characteristic of all Coleridge's thought: the search for a way of relating all events in a systematic pattern that is not static but progressive, and that manifests the balancing and interpenetration of the universal and the particular, order and individuality.[11] A true method, then, leads to a view of reality that is at once comprehensive, coherent, and dynamic. While it asserts the general, it must not annihilate the

7. Ibid., p. 415.
8. Ibid., p. 414.
9. Ibid., p. 417.
10. Ibid., p. 416.
11. Nearly all writers on Coleridge's general philosophy have made the same observation, which is hardly surprising. The relationship of "unity" to "multeity" and "individuation" is a constant Coleridgean theme. Some literary critics have found the same preoccupation central to Coleridge's poetry. According to one, Coleridge was driven by the need, common to all creative poets, to relate particular entities in life and nature with some underlying reality. See Frederick B. Rainsberry, "Coleridge and the Paradox of the Poetic Imperative," *Journal of English Literary History*, 21 (1954) 114–45. Another finds Coleridge's simultaneous yearning for the vast and affection for the little the keystone for analyzing the "Quantock" poems. See Louis Bonnerot, "The Two Worlds of Coleridge: some Aspects of his Attitude to Nature," *Essays by Divers Hands*, Transactions of the Royal Society of Literature, New Series, 28 (1956), 93–105.

particular. It must take account of the restless mutability of Nature and yet take care to expose the subtle harmony that governs change itself.

In his prospectus for the *Encyclopaedia Metropolitana*, Coleridge actually attempted to provide a methodical framework integrating all knowledge. What a symptom of intellectual decadence, Coleridge expostulated, that the alphabet should be regarded as the most appropriate way to organize human learning! He sought instead a less haphazard and arbitrary organizing framework of general principles around which all branches of learning could relate. His concern for method was not, of course, limited to this particular enterprise. Most of his intellectual life involved applying method to one field or another. Naturally all of his efforts were not equal in quality, but they do show a marked consistency of approach.

Concern for a general method was of course not unique to Coleridge. It was the primary preoccupation of all the great Romantic philosophers of his age. All had the intellectual heroism, presumption, or madness to search after principles that would integrate all knowledge. They believed that the true artist and philosopher, the truly creative mind, could dissolve and recast the bits and pieces of human insight into a comprehensive and unified vision of reality. They shared a great intolerance of partial views. Hence they felt justified in rejecting what they saw as the major strains of the Enlightenment—the rationalism typical of Descartes and the empiricism expressed so uncompromisingly by Hume. In the Romantic view, the Cartesian rationalists had achieved order by suppressing reality. They had ignored the damp vitality and surging energy of Nature and called the universe a machine. They postulated an orderly world of dead abstractions. The empiricists, on the other hand, had reduced the world to a jumbled aggregate of individualities, lacking any order or purpose. And both schools had collaborated on a psychology that reduced the half-divine mind of man to a supine receptacle of external sensation. A new philosophy was needed, one that would embrace all the richness and variety of life and yet point out its vital order and purpose. Metaphysics, religion, philosophy, physical science, psychology, aesthetics, and politics were to be brought methodically within a coherent vision of the world.

The Romantics looked for unity in all things because they expected to find it. There is no question of Coleridge's tendencies. Basil Willey described him accurately:

> The seminal principle, the original impulse, which was in him from childhood, was a sense of the Whole as a living unity, a sense of God in all and all in God, a faith in a divine spiritual activity as the ground of all existence. This faith never really left him, though it was obscured for a while by other influences, and modified in successive stages by his contacts with other minds. His great dread was lest, losing his wholeness of vision, he should be constrained to view the universe merely as an assemblage of parts, 'an immense heap of *little* things'.[12]

When Coleridge observed the world around him he saw not a meaningless jumble of particulars, but a shaping spirit. His religious instinct bade him "find tongues in trees; books in the running streams; sermons in stones; and good . . . in every thing."[13] He would sing with Blake: "Everything that lives is holy." For the Romantics all Nature was alive with divine energy —with Herder's *Kraft* or Hegel's World Spirit, or, in the Christian terms Coleridge preferred, with the divine Logos, the Word made flesh, the Son. Coleridge was filled with "a sort of sacred horror" as he meditated upon "this intuition of absolute existence"[14] which, he believed, could solve the age-old problem of epistemology—the separation of mind from matter.

Man is not isolated from the divine energy in Nature; it dwells within man himself: "the productive power, which in nature acts as nature, is essentially one (that is, of one kind) with the intelligence, which is in the human mind above nature."[15] Indeed, human perception is only possible because the material world and

---

12. Basil Willey, *Nineteenth Century Studies* (London, Chatto and Windus, 1949), p. 4.
13. Quoted by Coleridge, "The Friend," *Works*, 2, 449.
14. Ibid., p. 464.
15. Ibid., pp. 449–50.

the mind of man, the body and the spirit, are not alien substances, are not "absolutely heterogeneous, but *may* without any *absurdity* be supposed to be different modes, or degrees in perfection, of a common substratum."[16] The law of causality, Coleridge argued, holds only between homogeneous things, i.e. things having some common property. If the soul is only a *"thinking substance"* and the body a *"space-filling* substance," then it is impossible that *"esse,"* being, and *"scire,"* knowing, can ever unite. Human perception would be impossible.

Coleridge sought to discredit the whole Cartesian alienation of mind from body. For him both are a species of being linked by their sharing in the universal that is God. This communion makes man's perception of Nature possible. I see the world outside me because both my mind and the world share in the same divine energy and being. But my mind, unlike Nature, is conscious. It possesses the "Primary Imagination"—"the living Power and prime Agent of all human Perception." It is "a repetition in the finite mind of the eternal act of creation in the infinite I AM."[17]

The Primary Imagination is the fundamental faculty of the mind—the divine spark that gives man conscious awareness. But man's mind does more than merely reflect or passively register divine energy. Man possesses an active will of his own. If his mind is to achieve conscious understanding of the universe and of itself it must exercise its creative, poetic power to transform the Babel of outside impressions into a coherent language. This power is what Coleridge described as "the Secondary Imagination." It is an "echo" of the Primary "differing only in *degree,* and in the *mode* of its operation. It dissolves, diffuses, dissipates, in order to recreate; or where this process is rendered impossible, yet still at all events it struggles to idealize and to unify. It is essentially *vital,* even as all objects (*as* objects) are essentially fixed and dead."[18]

Imagination in this secondary sense is distinguished from "Fancy"—the mind as it collects and sorts ready-made impressions directly from the outside world or from memory. Fancy

16. Coleridge, *Biographia Literaria,* ed. John Shawcross (2 vols. Oxford, 1907), 1, 88.
17. Ibid., p. 202.
18. Ibid.

merely links the impressions without dissolving these fixed and dead counters into a new and more integrated unity. The distinction between Imagination and Fancy was designed primarily as a tool for literary analysis, for distinguishing between two kinds of poetry, between Dame Quickly and Hamlet. It implies, however, a more general philosophical distinction, and one at the very core of Coleridge's philosophy—the distinction between Reason and the Understanding. The two terms refer to two distinct types or levels of higher mental activity.

On the lower level, the human mind has an inborn tendency to classify and arrange its perceptions and to concentrate upon those aspects that divide and separate things from each other. Nature is seen as *natura naturata*—an immense heap of little things, cold and dead and ready to be sorted by the mind and placed in the appropriate jars. At this level of perception the mind sees itself as an active force, distinct from lifeless and mechanical Nature. At its higher level of awareness the mind perceives *natura naturans*, the vital force that informs Nature and links it to the energy present in man himself.

The Understanding is that lower aspect of the mind capable of comprehending *natura naturata*. The Understanding is "the conception of the sensuous, or the faculty by which we generalize and arrange the *phenomena* of perception."[19] It can arrange things according to categories and generalize from past experience. It can form only conceptions. Coleridge's distinction between a "conception" and an "Idea" illustrates the same attitude toward Nature and man's perception of it. A conception is a generalization formed *a posteriori* from past observations. An Idea, on the other hand, is an insight into a law or principle that governs the phenomena of Nature, that explains why certain phenomena must occur as they do. In this sense an Idea is more than a generalization from past experience. It is an intuitive insight into the essential nature of things. It is *a priori*. It is the tree waiting to emerge from the acorn.

Science governed by the Understanding alone is capable only

19. Coleridge, "The Friend," *Works*, 2, 145. I have used *The Friend* rather than the later *Aids to Reflections* because in the former Coleridge was specifically concerned with relating his general philosophical ideas to politics.

of an endless collection of facts without any knowledge of the basic "laws" that govern these facts and indeed make them necessary rather than accidental. Coleridge has nothing but contempt for the empiricist positivism of such writers as Bentham. To Coleridge the positivist is a scientific Dame Quickly. His research lacks any leading Idea. He refuses to get beneath the surface of events to the moving forces that cause them. The empiricist historian believes that writing and understanding history can be accomplished merely by an industrious compiling of facts. The same empiricist method applied to natural science results only in the aimless accumulation of more and more data.

But science, according to Coleridge, is not merely concerned with the haphazard collection of facts; true science seeks information that is significant. Information becomes significant when it leads the mind to an insight into the laws that govern the universe. The great scientists—the Galileos and Newtons—were interested not in information for its own sake, but in the laws that give order to the natural world. To be sure, they experimented. True science, Coleridge held, can never be the arbitrary tyranny of the mind over matter. Knowledge of individual facts is of course essential. The general theory cannot ignore the particular fact. But research in particulars must ultimately lead to something general if it is to be true science. It is only a proper method that keeps the mind from being lost either in details or in unreal abstractions.

At the level of the Understanding, the mind cannot attain a truly scientific knowledge of the world. For such knowledge the Understanding must be illumined by "Reason." Pure Reason, as defined by Coleridge, is the mental organ by which man perceives the universal, the eternal, and the necessary fundamental truths of logic, morality, and religion. In the philosophical and moral spheres pure Reason is formal and rather simple. In logic, for example, it is essentially the law of contradiction upon which all formal logic is ultimately built. In the moral sphere Reason is the awareness that one ought not to perform actions one would think wrong if performed by another.

Coleridge believed that men are essentially equal in the possession of pure Reason. Pure Reason is something like the Primary Imagination—a universal attribute of all human life. But pure

Reason alone, like the Primary Imagination, is of little practical use in comprehending or controlling the actual world in which man lives. To be effective pure Reason must coalesce with the Understanding. When the distinct powers of each are united, there results the "scientific faculty." "Reason therefore, in this secondary sense, and used, not as a spiritual organ, but as a faculty, namely, the understanding or soul enlightened by that organ,—reason, [in this sense] . . . or the scientific faculty, is the intellection of the possibility or essential properties of things by means of the laws that constitute them."[20] Only by the aid of Reason is man's Understanding capable of getting beneath the surface to the essential character and necessity of phenomena, to the "Ideas" that govern all things. What is true of natural science is true of moral and political science as well. Thus it is Reason that makes man's highest achievements possible, that raises him above the animals.

While Coleridge heaped scorn upon those positivists who would base knowledge on the Understanding alone, he was equally vehement in emphasizing the impotence and irrelevancy of pure Reason when detached from the Understanding. Neither man's world nor his own human nature can be comprehended by pure Reason alone. Men are not uniform creatures of predictable rationality any more than the physical universe is made up of ideal geometrical forms. In man as in Nature, universal Reason is clothed in an infinite number of recalcitrant particulars. Only God is pure Reason. It is the Understanding that is the essence of man. Sense pours in impressions from the outside world. The Understanding collects and sorts these impressions. The divine light of Reason shines in from above. In the illumination of Reason, the Understanding strives toward comprehension of itself and the world, and of the laws that govern both. But Reason cannot exist in man apart from the Understanding. Coleridge expressed the relationship in religious terms:

> God is the Identity of Reason and Being, and of both with the Eternal *Word*, the only-begotten Son. Reason is . . . the Light of the Son, the Light which the Son *is*—and this the Light, that lighteth every man that cometh into the World—

20. Ibid., pp. 146–47.

Now the Understanding is the Man himself, contemplated as an intelligent Creature—and the Light shineth down into his natural darkness (= blind instinct) and by its' presence converts the vital instinct into Understanding—and this Light of the Understanding, or this Understanding as modified by this Light, may be distinguished from the Reason itself, as *Lumen* from *Lux*. It is the *Lumen* Humanum a Luce Divina and the implanted susceptibility of this *Illumination* so that the Light is present *for* him as well as in him, is present as *Light*—constitutes him a *Man*, and is truly the *Image* of God for Lumen est *imago* Lucis.

The Understanding . . . *is* the Man—whose rationality consists in the innate susceptibility of the Lumen a Luce—but the Reason is not the man.[21]

Reason is always in man and in that sense might be considered an attribute of his humanity. Still "the necessity of Sleep reminds him of his Fall by the periodical eclipse of the Light."

In brief, God shines his Reason upon all men equally. But Reason can only exist for man within the human Understanding. Man, then, is never pure Reason. Thus it is that while Reason is one and universal, the mind of each man is always unique and particular. While all men are equal in their possession of the essential truths of pure Reason, they are far from equal in that "scientific faculty" that applies these universals to illuminate the particular perceptions of the Understanding. In a similar vein, while it might be said that all men are essentially equal in their Primary Imagination, it cannot be denied that they are far from equal in their Secondary. All men see and feel, yet all are not poets. Similarly all men may intuit the categorical imperative or know that a straight line is the shortest distance between two points, but not all men are moral philosophers or geometers. Men share sense and Reason, but they are far from equal in those active powers of the mind by which these common faculties are employed. In short, men are not equal in their ability to gain knowledge of the world in which they live.

Coleridge constantly asserted that the distinction between Reason and Understanding was the very essence of his philosophy.

21. Notebook 47, fol. 22ᵛ, 23ʳ, and 23ᵛ.

And indeed it is. The distinction illustrates two tendencies of his general philosophy that were of the greatest importance in shaping his political thought. The first was his preoccupation, common to so many Romantics, with the problem of maintaining a dynamic balance between the particular and the universal, individuality and coherence. The second was his emphasis on the active role of the mind in perceiving reality and the unequal degree to which men possess these active faculties. The first tendency made him a constitutionalist, the second an aristocrat.

When Coleridge imagined the universe, he saw not a dead heap of uniform particles governed by simple, invariable, and mechanical laws. His universe was a vast arena filled with squirming, individual particulars, each with a vitality and purpose of its own. Yet there is a divine energy—a shaping spirit that coaxes individual inclination into general purpose. Nature is not like a machine, but an organism made up of many individual parts, each with its own character and function, and yet all participating in a larger unity. Like an organism, Nature is governed by a balance of opposite forces—an equilibrium that must itself reflect the progressive growth of the whole. When man applies his mind to the study of Nature, he must be careful to lose sight neither of the general laws nor of the particular parts. He must employ, in short, both his Reason and his Understanding.

This way of looking at the world has numerous advantages when applied to the study of the modern constitutional State. When Coleridge looked at the social universe, he never expected to find a tidy arrangement of uniform individual particles. When he found society to consist of a disorderly aggregate of quite distinct groups—each with its own individual interests, habits, and values—he was not surprised or uncomfortable. Such, after all, was the very nature of reality. Yet Coleridge might also be expected to have possessed special acuteness in ferreting out the subtle forces that hold a society together and give it direction and coherence. A tolerance for individuality and diversity, combined with a keen eye for the principles that harmonize and reconcile, is the very essence of constitutionalism. These were traits possessed not only by Coleridge, but by many of the great Romantic philosophers of his age. It is no more surprising that some of these writers are notable for their study of the constitutional

State, I suspect, than it is entirely coincidental that Beethoven, with a similar program in music, achieved so striking an expansion of the symphonic form.

Romantic writers did not, of course, invent or even revive constitutionalism. The doctrine of checks and balances was never more in vogue than during the Enlightenment. No one, for example, could have been more insistent than Paine on the necessity for a written constitution spelling out an apparatus of powers and guarantees. But numerous examples from actual political systems make it clear that a formal constitution is no guarantee against tyranny. Certainly most observers would agree with Tocqueville and J. S. Mill that democratic rule of the majority is not in itself necessarily a secure safeguard for individual and group liberties. Constitutional rights and powers are more firmly based when accompanied by pluralism, by a genuine perception of and appreciation for social diversity. Both Coleridge and Burke had an extraordinarily sensitive view of the realities of political life. They saw and were delighted by the diverse complexity of a traditional society. They possessed that gothic love for detail typical of so many Romantics. While it may have blunted their sensitivity to the need for extending new rights or curbing excessive old ones, it did make them appreciate and guard jealously the constitutional freedom they already had. And their Romantic vision, I am suggesting, gave them not only a wonderful sense of the details of political life, but allowed them to apprehend the shaping spirit within, the forces that maintain coherence and unity throughout such diversity.

Coleridge's philosophical principles urged him not only toward a pluralistic constitutionalism, but to aristocracy as well. Poets and philosophers are not the only people who need a capacity for vision. States should be ruled by men who possess political Imagination, whose Understandings, illuminated by Reason, have achieved an adequate grasp of the real world of politics. Since all men are not equal in their practicing Reason, all men cannot be statesmen any more than all men can be poets. Mrs. Quickly could not rule the State. She lacked the power to see Reason through the particulars. At best, she might muddle through. Hamlet would be no better. He was dominated by his manic preoccupation with a personal world of abstractions. Like the mad Jacobin reformer, he was cut off from the diverse world of particulars in which other men live. Both Hamlet and Mrs. Quickly would be deficient in their political Imaginations. Both lacked the "esemplastic power" to create an adequate vision of reality. Balanced insight is not commonplace and requires careful education for its development. Hence the well-ordered State must inevitably be led by the few and not by the many.

Coleridge's emphasis upon the active powers of the mind runs contrary to a third tendency present in his thought and in Romantics generally—the tendency toward pantheism and fatalism —fatalism because divine energy determines all that happens, and pantheism because this *Kraft* is the stuff not only of the mind but of matter as well. Coleridge recognized both tendencies in his solution to the problem of knowledge, disapproved, and was much troubled.[22] He acknowledged that, while his system illustrated the necessity of a God who is absolute being itself, it failed to show why this God is in any way distinct from the universe. He confessed that the philosophical school he espoused, followed to its logical conclusion, led inevitably to pantheism. And if the individuality of God is swallowed up in the totality of the universe, why not the individuality of man as well? How can the notion of a divine spirit shaping all that occurs be resolved with the notion of individual free will? And what of evil? If all is the result of divine *Kraft*, how can there be right and wrong? For these dilemmas, Coleridge admitted no purely philosophical solutions. But, he argued, man has a deeper insight than the dia-

22. A. O. Lovejoy, in "Coleridge and Kant's Two Worlds," *English Literary History*, 7 (1940), argued that the whole distinction between Reason and the Understanding was used by Coleridge chiefly for "vindicating philosophically man's moral freedom and accountability" (p. 341). In Lovejoy's opinion, Coleridge did not so much abandon Hartley's necessitarianism—to which he once adhered—as seek another world where it did not apply. The Imagination was no solution. It merely substituted the determinism caused by man's internal psychological nature for that caused by external impressions. Freedom could be found only in the noumenal world. But even here, Lovejoy argues, Coleridge, deeply conscious of his own sinfulness, believed an omnipotent God had created man with a propensity to sin. Therefore Coleridge never could establish man's absolute undetermined freedom, and the chief purpose for making the distinction between Reason and the Understanding was not and could not be fulfilled.

lectical intellect. Philosophy alone inevitably leads man to "a chasm which the moral being only, which the spirit and religion of man alone can fill up."[23]

This elevation of the spirit above the semblances of custom and the senses to a world of spirit, this life in the idea, even in the supreme and godlike, which alone merits the name

23. Coleridge, "The Friend," *Works*, 2, 471. In this instance at least Coleridge might seem to escape from what René Wellek asserts to be his fundamental weakness as a professional philosopher: "Coleridge has little insight into the incompatibility of different trends of thought . . . Coleridge's structure has here a storey from Kant, there a part of a room from Schelling, there a roof from Anglican theology." René Wellek, *Immanuel Kant in England, 1793–1838* (Princeton, Princeton University Press, 1931), p. 67.

In a larger sense, however, the passage supports Wellek's fundamental charge that Coleridge, while seeking to construct an "ontology in the old sense" but with an "idealistic technique," mistakenly used Kant for this purpose and eventually gave up the effort to reconcile, accepted a dualism of the head and the heart, took refuge in "immediate knowledge and faith," and hence finished as "a prophet of the end and failure of Reason" (pp. 134–35). Wellek's general conclusion was supported by Elizabeth Winkelmann, *Coleridge und die Kantische Philosophie* (Leipsig, Mayer and Müller, 1933), who stressed Coleridge's similarities to the German votary of feeling over intellect, F. H. Jacobi. The tie with Jacobi is examined in W. Schrickx, "Coleridge and Friedrich Heinrich Jacobi," *Revue Belge de Philologie et d'Histoire, 36* (1958), 812–50.

J. H. Muirhead takes issue with Wellek and Winkelmann in "Metaphysician or Mystic," *Coleridge: Studies by Several Hands*, ed. Edmund Blunden and Earl Leslie Griggs (London, 1934). Muirhead places Coleridge not with those who deny reason in matters of the heart, but among those who examine what is meant by reason and its function in human experience. Coleridge's intuition was "the completion of thought returning to the intuitions of sense with all the richness and variety which its passage through the prism of reflective mind had given it" (p. 192). Muirhead compares the Coleridgean development of Kantian dualism to Hegel.

Another critic asserts that Coleridge was a mystic who sought "to explain in terms of contemporary science and psychology areas of experience which older writers had recognized but which they had discussed and interpreted in ways no longer acceptable." Richard Haven, "Coleridge, Hartley, and the Mystics," *Journal of the History of Ideas, 20* (1959) 494. Coleridge's particular problem was how to be a mystic "without feeling that he was a mere enthusiast" (p. 478).

An interesting observation concerning the question whether Coleridge was a fideist or a rationalist comes in W. Schrickx, "An Unnoticed Note of Coleridge's on Kant," *Neophilologus, 42* (1958), 147–51. As a journalist and political and religious thinker, Coleridge was deeply involved in the

of life, and without which our organic life is but a state of somnambulism; this it is which affords the sole sure anchorage in the storm, and at the same time the substantiating principle of all true wisdom, the satisfactory solution of all the contradiction of human nature, of the whole riddle of the world. This alone belongs to and speaks intelligibly to all alike, the learned and the ignorant, if but the heart listens.[24]

To confirm his faith in a personal God and in his own free will, man must accept the insights of his own religious sense. Coleridge believed that philosophy will always need to be supplemented by religious faith. To be sure, philosophy may advance. The intellect may come more and more to comprehend in science what was once known only in faith. For Coleridge these advancements are the noblest chapters in the history of human achievement. But mysteries will always remain which only the heart can unlock. The philosopher who scorns faith may well be less wise than the simple man who listens to the true instincts of his own nature.

"issues which divide communities." He was similar to a modern existentialist in his desire to "revitalize through genuine experience what has been dead matter for so long" (p. 150).

This seems a point worth noting. In discussing the excellences and shortcomings of Coleridge the philosopher, it should be remembered that he was, in his way, intensely concerned with the great practical issues of his day. He was first and last a preacher. He tried to write for a popular rather than professional audience. Some of his greatest philosophical treatises are attempts to relate general principles to particular current controversies, e.g. *Church and State* and *Theory of Life*. And he believed, above all, that the greatest danger in the practical world comes from those who take too narrow a view of reality, from those who rely too exclusively upon one type of insight into truth. In my opinion, that is his most impressive characteristic as a political theorist. It is certainly proper and profitable to criticize his powers as a philosophical system-builder. That does not however do justice to the extraordinary imaginative insight and good sense with which he analyzed the philosophical implications of practical issues and institutions. Any evaluation of Coleridge purely as a builder of philosophical systems is likely, in Miss Coburn's words, to miss a "total, complicated, subtle, unsystematic, illuminating vision of him, as a functional human being and thinker." Foreword to I. A. Richards, *Coleridge on Imagination* (Bloomington, Ind., 1960), p. xvi.

24. Coleridge, "The Friend," *Works*, 2, 471–72.

It would be a mistake, I believe, to draw the conclusion that Coleridge was an anti-intellectual, "Romantic" votary of feeling rather than intellect.[25] He was in a predicament not uncommon to a sensitive and philosophical mind. He firmly held to a number of apparently irreconcilable ideas. He believed in a divine energy, reflected in the human spirit, that shaped a progressively developing universe. The inevitable direction of this belief, he admitted, was toward pantheism and fatalism. This side of his thought is reflected in his definition of Primary Imagination. On the other hand, he was deeply committed to Christian and humanist traditions. He believed in a personal God, and he believed in the individuality and free will of men. Hence he believed in the existence not only of a moral order, but of moral choice open to the individual. He could scarcely therefore believe that "WHATEVER IS, IS RIGHT." Man is able to choose evil as well as good. The human mind is active and free. There is a creative, as well as a primal Imagination.

Coleridge tried all his life to work out a reconciliation. He had the honesty and courage to confess that only faith could finally bridge the void between these two sets of beliefs. Yet he would abandon neither. To do so he would have had to deny the fundamental intuitions of his spirit. He preferred to confess his intellectual shortcomings rather than abandon his faith.

But Coleridge was far from wishing to assert the superiority of feeling to intellect. Indeed the whole practice of making a sharp separation between the two is contrary to the spirit of his philosophy. He believed that the intellect of man, to reach the fullness of its power, must be infused with the insights of religious and moral faith. These insights, after all, are real for man. They are

25. As a political theorist, Coleridge cannot easily be accused of anti-intellectualism. On the one hand he specifically criticized Burke for exalting feeling over rationality and thus making it possible to justify the most absurd and wicked prejudices. On the other hand he criticized Rousseau's theory of politics as relying upon intuitive and immediate "Reason" which was, in Coleridge's opinion, an inadequate guide to practical action until mingled with the reflective faculty of Understanding. (See Ch. 4.) Finally, Coleridge's most original contribution to political theory was perhaps his notion of a National Church, vital to the political health of the nation and defined not as a religious, but as an educational institution. (See Ch. 7, p. 136 ff.)

part of what Bergson later called the immediate data of consciousness. There is no sound philosophical reason for regarding them
as less real than the data presented by the physical sciences. The
intellect, when separated artificially from these insights, is seduced into partial views that are caricatures of the fullness of
reality. The greatest weakness of the intellect, Coleridge believed,
is its tendency to seize arbitrarily upon one type of insight and to
suppress all others. Man has several ways of knowing truth. The
philosophical mind must remain open to them all. Yet the mind
of man, to perceive truth, requires more than a simple infusion of
faith. It is the never-ending task of the intellect to seek to unify
the various kinds of perception even while admitting the impos-
sibility of final solutions.

It is interesting to speculate how the contrasting philosophical
tendencies indicated in the two kinds of Imagination may have
been reflected in political theory. One appears to imply government by an intellectual aristocracy. What of the other? If the
Primary Imagination reflects pantheism, emotionalism, and fatalism, how were these qualities expressed in Romantic political
theory? Surely they are found in Carlyle's doctrine of the hero.
And perhaps in Rousseau's general will, which he believed was
most likely to be honored in the spontaneous decisions of the un-
reflecting majority. Rousseau, of course, was careful to make
the distinction between the general will and the will of all. But
for the enthusiasts of democracy, it was easy to combine them
both with the Romantic World Spirit or *Kraft* and thus argue
that the voice of the people was the voice of God. In either case
the favored group, heroes or masses, possesses a special insight
into the divine will, an insight based not upon intellect, but upon
immediate intuitive knowledge.

Coleridge's political theory is dominated by an opposing tendency. His emphasis upon the necessity for an active disciplined
intellect to perceive truth, upon the Secondary Imagination, led
him, like Plato, to faith in an educated aristocracy. It could be
said, I suppose, that as the older Coleridge became politically conservative, he ceased to be a "Romantic." This assumes that the
Secondary Imagination was less Romantic than the Primary. But
is this assumption justified? The opposing tendencies reflected in
each coexisted uneasily in most of the major figures of the Ro-

mantic movement. Perhaps it is arbitrary to declare one tendency Romantic and the other not. The cardinal tenet of Romantic philosophy was that every truth contains its opposite. This was the Romantic formula for avoiding partial views of reality. Perhaps it should be taken more seriously by those who study Romantic thought.

CHAPTER 3

The Romantic Context

The terms "Romantic" and "Romanticism" have now been used several times in discussing Coleridge's general philosophy. This usage is sufficiently unusual to call for an explanation. It would be too Coleridgean to become involved here in a protracted discussion of Romanticism and thus annihilate whatever coherent train of thought the preceding chapters may possess. Nevertheless, the question of what the characteristics of Romantic thought were is relevant to an appreciation of Coleridge's political ideas.[1] For Coleridge was not an isolated phenomenon; he was part of a major intellectual and spiritual revolution that has dominated much of modern culture and whose general effects are just beginning to be grasped by historians of ideas. If there was any movement in the nineteenth century that occupied the same role as the Enlightenment in the eighteenth, it was Romanticism. Indeed it is possible to see much of the cultural history of the nineteenth century as the rise, disintegration, and decay of the Romantic world-view, the effects of which extend well into our century.

Romanticism has long been used as a concept in the separate histories of literature, art, or music, where it has generally been defined more narrowly than in the history of ideas. Romanticism has been seen in terms of this or that particular school of writers or musicians which produced, for a generation or two, works that

1. I discuss Romanticism in order to suggest the larger cultural context within which Coleridge moved. What I believe to be especially relevant is the possible affinity between Romanticism and constitutionalism—a point perhaps not so often made as others in this chapter.

unquestionably displayed genius, but were perhaps flawed for modern taste by their characteristic emotional extravagance. The word "romantic" descends from the French *roman* (OF. *romant*), a vague form originally implying a tale written in the vulgar tongue rather than in Latin, usually in prose, and generally dealing with the heroic, amorous, supernatural, or extravagantly picturesque. Every culture has features regarded as "romantic," meaning in some way exotic and undisciplined.

As a concept in the history of ideas, Romanticism is generally regarded as a way of looking at the world that grew up in opposition to the dominant world-view of the Enlightenment. More specifically it refers to a particular cultural movement that began to flourish first in Germany, where it is associated with such famous figures of the later eighteenth century as Jacobi, Lessing, Herder, and Goethe. A recognizable Romantic movement also grew up in England well before the turn of the century, where it is frequently connected with such names as Blake, Wordsworth, Southey, Burke, and, of course, Coleridge.

Like every other major intellectual movement, Romanticism had origins in the past. Rousseau was a strong and immediate inspiration. "Romantic" influences have been traced from such diverse sources as Shaftesbury, the Cambridge Platonists, Leibnitz, Spinoza, and German Pietism. Hume unconsciously served the cause of Romanticism by effectively eroding the rationalistic presuppositions of the Enlightenment. The same can be said for Kant, whose philosophical system was transformed by the Romantics for their own purposes.

As is usual in the study of ideas, the chief difficulty with Romanticism is defining it. While the Enlightenment was, of course, infinitely more varied and complex than the caricature invented by the Romantics, there is nevertheless some relative measure of agreement on its basic tenets. No such consensus exists on Romanticism. To begin with, the word itself is loaded with all sorts of extraneous connotations. Like the word liberal, it is extremely vague. It has similarly become, for many, a term automatically denoting praise or abuse. Even as employed in cultural history, it can, like "classical" or "mannerist," be applied to certain stages within every period. A. O. Lovejoy has taken the ultimate step and argued that the word is so compromised as to be useless, and should be exorcised from our vocabulary.[2] Other students of the period have sought to rescue the term by changing it to "Romanticist"—perhaps a useful, but assuredly an unattractive alteration.[3]

In addition to the difficulties attached to the word, the Romantics themselves were extremely complex personalities. It is impossible to derive from them an "orthodox" Romanticism. They placed great store upon what was individual and spontaneous, and hence are recalcitrant subjects for general definitions. Their philosophy often saw reality as a delicate balance of discordant opposites—a notion that contributed greatly to the comprehensiveness of their thought, but not to its clarity. Accordingly the Romantics are particularly vulnerable to the misunderstandings that arise from excessive generalization and abstraction. The various elements often regarded as typically Romantic are generally profoundly affected by the way a particular author combines them. It is therefore hazardous to single out of context some one element as typical of one or all Romantics. The essence of Romantic thought often lies in the balance and not in the elements taken by themselves. In spite of all these difficulties, the term is still in use. It does suggest a means of relating diverse phenomena in politics, literature, philosophy, and the arts, and hence achieving a comprehensive insight into modern Western culture.

Perhaps it will be useful to set down some of the elements that have been found to be typically Romantic. For all the reasons just

2. A. O. Lovejoy, "On the Discrimination of Romanticisms," *Essays in the History of Ideas* (Baltimore, 1948), pp. 228–53. The same point could, of course, be made about the Enlightenment. Anyone accustomed to seeing that period exclusively in terms of the image of it created by the Romantics should read Ernst Cassirer, *The Philosophy of the Enlightenment* (Princeton, Princeton University Press, 1951).

It is quite clear that there were numerous "Romantic" strains in the Enlightenment. The more precisely one studies cultural history, the greater the inclination to do away with labels entirely. Yet, as I suggest, to renounce such generalizations altogether robs cultural history of much of its possible relevance to contemporary thought.

3. For a definition and justification of the term, see Jacques Barzun, *Classic, Romantic, and Modern* (Garden City, 1961), Ch. I, "Romanticism— Dead or Alive?" The word "Romanticist" has long been in use. The *O.E.D.* finds it as early as 1830—in *Blackwell's Magazine*, 27, 317.

mentioned, such a list can be only hypothetical—a guide to help in framing relevant questions, rather than in answering them definitely. For however one defines Romanticism, no Romantic will always be Romantic. A general definition can hope only to describe what was predominantly Romantic. In the history of ideas the more abstract and coherent a general definition is, the less likely it is to apply to anyone in particular. The dilemma is inescapable if ideas are to be discussed in relation to particular men.

To begin with, it is generally agreed that Romanticism was a reaction against the Neo-Classical literary and artistic taste of the Enlightenment. Where the Enlightenment preferred formally prescribed rules of art, the Romantics praised spontaneity and individualism. The man of the Enlightenment tended to admire polish, order, rationality, and self-control. The Romantic preferred vigorous emotion, soaring enthusiasm, and picturesque disorder. The "Revolt" of the early Romantics was animated by two basic concerns: the desire for artistic freedom or "individuality," and a profound interest in the irrational and emotional aspects of human behavior and experience.

Individuality is an elusive concept. Perhaps it would be more helpful to say that the Romantics were, like medieval nominalists, interested in particulars and suspicious of generalizations. They were especially impatient with generalizations that could be transformed into laws hindering the creative freedom of the artist. The world-view of the Enlightenment encouraged men to seek general laws summarizing some aspect of what was believed to be an unchanging natural order. Newton discovered the laws of physics. Others sought to achieve equal authority in different fields. In the arts, Neo-Classical taste ran always to "Rules." But the Romantics were more interested in exceptions than in rules, in the bizarre than in the commonplace. They flouted the established artistic conventions and felt that only by so doing could they express the fullness of their own individual vision and genius. It became apparent, however, as the "Revolt" matured, that it was not so much against all order and form as against the particular creed and taste of the Enlightenment. Coleridge and Wordsworth, for example, can scarcely be accused of lack of interest in critical rules in general. But Romantics were incensed at those Enlightened critics who had applied their particular Rules to the great literature of the past and found it inferior because of its irregularities. Voltaire's dismissal of Shakespeare as a talented but uncouth barbarian seemed particularly outrageous. To the Romantics the canons of the Enlightenment were not true universals reflecting some fundamental order of things, but the arbitrary conventions by which an arrogant and rather unpoetic age sought to impose its taste upon both the past and the future.

The appreciation for individuality was extended not only to particular artists, but also to separate cultures. It is not surprising that it was a Romantic, Herder, who developed modern historicism and cultural relativism.[4] The natural tendency of the Enlightenment was to pick a single cosmopolitan ideal culture and to regard all others as promising or retrograde in terms of their distance from the ideal. As a result of this mode of proceeding, whole nations and periods were cast outside the pale of civilization. Herder, on the contrary, believed that each *Volk* possesses its own individual form of genius. Who can say, Herder argued, that one culture or one age is better than another? The task for the critic and historian is to understand each civilization on its own individual terms, not to judge it by external standards. Herder's teaching was among other things both a justification for his interest in folk literature and an effort to free German culture from its bondage to the Enlightened French.

The typical Romantic appreciation for individuality was closely and naturally connected with great interest in the irrational and emotional aspects of human experience, a preoccupation often dubbed the Revolt against Reason. For the Enlightenment, Reason was a universal which all men shared and which thus served to make all men alike in their tastes and judgments. It was when men were guided by their emotions and behaved "unreasonably" that they developed the peculiar notions and beliefs that divide

4. Herder was one of the most typical and complete Romantics. His great comprehensive work was *Ideen zur Philosophie der Geschichte der Menscheit* (4 vols. Riga and Leipzig, 1784–91). He was the first to use the word "culture" (*Kultur*) in its modern sense. See Robert T. Clark, Jr., *Herder, His Life and Thought* (Berkeley and Los Angeles, University of California Press, 1955) and Martin Schütze, "The Fundamental Ideas in Herder's Thought," *Modern Philology*, 18 (1920–21), 65–78 and 289–302; 19 (1921–22), 113–30 and 361–82; 21 (1923–24), 29–48 and 113–32.

mankind. While the Enlightenment thus taught men to shun the irrational dimension of life, the Romantics sought to explore it fully. For the Romantic there was often a deeper truth to be found through intuition and feeling than from abstract philosophical reasoning. This characteristic is perhaps most clearly illustrated in the eighteenth century by the *Sturm und Drang* period of German literature and the epistemological theories of Jacobi and his followers.

Romantic concern with the irrational and the unusual sometimes encouraged strikingly marked theatrical flamboyance in the private behavior of several of the leading figures of the movement. It is sometimes overlooked, however, that the eccentricities of an artist are not necessarily reflected in his work. Indeed, many of the Romantics are notable not only for impressive technical mastery of their art, but for an astonishing quantity of work turned out during lives that were often brief as well as tumultuous. Coleridge is an excellent example. His life may have been untidy, but his poetry does not suffer from a lack of craftsmanship.

The preoccupation of early Romantics with the emotional and irrational was not a superficial and transitory enthusiasm. It points to what is perhaps their most salient characteristic: their belief in a spiritual force that animates all things. All creation is infused with divine energy that gives life, form, and purpose to the universe. Furthermore, man can communicate with this divine energy. Wordsworth found the divine in nature. For Blake "Everything that lives is holy." Herder found *Kraft* everywhere —in Nature and in the spirit of a free people through history.[5]

We have already seen the tendency toward pantheism in Coleridge and the difficulties it caused him.[6] While several other Romantics, including even Herder, denied that they were pantheists, they nevertheless generally saw God as an immanent force animating the universe, rather than as a distinct being outside creation. Thus for them the Divine was essentially on earth and not in heaven. Although Romantics placed great emphasis on what could be called a "religious" sense, and although many of them

5. See J. G. von Herder, *Gott . . . Einige Gespräche über Spinoza's System* (1787).
6. See Ch. 2, pp. 41 ff.

developed an enthusiastic appreciation for the aesthetic and corporate traditions of the Church, their world-view was at heart incompatible wth orthodox Christianity. Not only did individual Romantics reject particular dogmas like Original Sin, but the whole Romantic notion of the deity could not be reconciled with the traditional Christian creed. Romanticism was a new modern religion. Later revivals of Christianity, like the Oxford Movement, however much they owed to the new prestige Romanticism had given religious feeling, could not be Romantic as long as they were Christian in any traditional sense.

The Romantic search for the divine often turned inward, instead of to Nature or history. Schelling, for example, spoke of a higher state of "self-consciousness" in which the individual could escape from the categories of sense and become one with the eternal vital force of Being that was the basic reality of all existence.[7] Bergson introduced much the same notion into twentieth-

7. See Friedrich W. J. von Schelling, *System of Transcendental Idealism* (1800). The uncited resemblance to Schelling of Coleridge's thought and even phraseology in Chapter 12 of the *Biographia Literaria* is notorious. The import of this similarity can at least be qualified. To begin with, Coleridge was speaking in Chapter 12 as much as an historian or analyst of ideas as an original philosopher. He attempted to sketch two fundamental approaches to the problem of knowledge that divide philosophers into two basic schools. He does not claim to be the founder of either school, but merely summarizes two points of view. In Chapter 9 of the *Biographia Literaria*, Coleridge acknowledged his debt to Schelling: "In Schelling's 'NATUR-PHILOSOPHIE,' and the 'SYSTEM DES TRANSCENDENTALEN IDEALISMUS,' I first found a genial coincidence with much that I had toiled out for myself, and a powerful assistance in what I had yet to do." He went on to assert, however, that:

> an identity of thought, or even similarity of phrase, will not be at all times a certain proof that the passage has been borrowed from Schelling, or that the conceptions were originally learnt from him. In this instance, as in the dramatic lectures of Schlegel to which I have before alluded, from the same motive of self-defence against the charge of plagiarism, many of the most striking resemblances, indeed all the main and fundamental ideas, were born and matured in my mind before I had ever seen a single page of the German Philosopher; and I might indeed affirm with truth, before the more important works of Schelling had been written, or at least made public. Nor is this coincidence at all to be wondered at. We had studied in the same school; been disciplined by the same preparatory philosophy, namely, the

century thought with his theory of biological evolution.[8]

Naturally the Romantics believed that to perceive the workings of indwelling divine energy—whether in Nature, history, or man —was to grasp the highest form of truth, the most significant aspect of reality. Perception of this truth, however, required more than the usual powers of rational human understanding. To plumb the mysteries of the universe, a higher intuitive insight

---

writings of Kant; we had both equal obligations to the polar logic and dynamic philosophy of Giordano Bruno; and Schelling has lately, and as of recent acquisition, avowed that same affectionate reverence for the labours of Behmen, and other mystics, which I had formed at a much earlier period. The coincidence of SCHELLING's system with certain general ideas of Behmen, he declares to have been *mere* coincidence; while *my* obligations have been more direct. *He* needs give to Behmen only feelings of sympathy; while I owe him a debt of gratitude. God forbid! that I should be suspected of a wish to enter into a rivalry with Schelling for the honours so unequivocally his right, not only as a great and original genius, but as the *founder* of the PHILOSOPHY OF NATURE, and as the most successful *improver* of the Dynamic System which, begun by Bruno, was re-introduced (in a more philosophical form, and freed from all its impurities and visionary accompaniments) by KANT; in whom it was the native and necessary growth of his own system.

(*Biographia Literaria*, ed. Shawcross, *1*, 102–04)

Donald Hirsch's study of the similarities between Wordsworth's ideas and Schelling's doctrines from 1797 to 1806—a period in which scholars generally agree neither Wordsworth nor Coleridge knew anything of Schelling—tends to strengthen Coleridge's assertion of independence. See E. Donald Hirsch, Jr., *Wordsworth and Schelling*, Yale Studies in English, 145 (New Haven, Yale University Press, 1960).

Perhaps the last word belongs to Schelling. Professor Hirsch points out a long footnote in which Schelling expressed his admiration for Coleridge's understanding of philosophy in general and the relation of philosophy to mythology in particular. He poked fun at the British for their criticism of Coleridge's unacknowledged use of his terms and implied that Coleridge's countrymen were so materialistically minded that they regarded concepts and terms in philosophy as if they were technological inventions, jealously to be guarded from competitors. As far as Schelling was concerned: "Einem wirklich congenialen Mann sollte man dergleichen nicht anrechnen." F. W. J. von Schelling, "Einleitung in die Philosophie der Mythologie," *Sämmtliche Werke*, ed. K. F. A. Schelling (14 vols. Stuttgart and Augsburg, 1856), *1*, 196.

8. A. O. Lovejoy, *The Reason, the Understanding, and Time* (Baltimore, The Johns Hopkins Press, 1961).

was needed. Hence the distinction in Coleridge between the higher intuitive powers of the mind which, he felt, should properly be called "Reason," and the normal rational powers of the mind, or the "Understanding."

Emphasis upon direct more than merely rational insight could mean, as Kant feared, the substitution of spontaneous and undisciplined intuition for rigorous philosophical analysis.[9] But the faculty of spontaneous intuition turned out in many cases to be less destructive of more traditional forms of rationality than Kant had predicted. Reason, for the more philosophically minded of the Romantics, often bore something of the same relation to the Understanding as, in the Thomist synthesis, the truths of revelation bore to those of natural law. Not all the Romantics, for example, believed that the scientist should abandon his laboratory for long introspective walks in the country. Indeed, some leading literary figures of the movement, Coleridge and Goethe for example, were remarkably well informed about the scientific thought of their day. Rather the Romantic believed that routine experimentation would never reveal significant truth unless illumined by intuitive inspiration. Thus the Romantics transformed their initial interest in the irrational into a full-fledged epistemological theory, more complex but certainly no less "philosophical" than the corresponding theories of the Enlightenment against which they revolted.

The Romantic doctrine of Reason gave a new prestige to the creative artist. Since imagination was indispensable to the perception of significant knowledge, the unusual sensitivity of a poet or artist could command an insight into the real nature of things that might be denied to a less imaginative scientist. Not only might the artist possess superior vision of the indwelling divine presence in all things, but poetry or art might well be a more satisfactory means of expressing that vision. Hence the Romantic belief in the political "hero." Certain men, because of their un-

9. Kant voiced his fears in a famous article *Von einem neuerdings erhobenen vornehmen Ton in der Philosophie* in the *Berliner Monatsschrift* of May 1796. The relationship of Kant to the German Romantics is discussed in Lovejoy, *The Reason*, Lecture I, passim. Whether Kant's criticism should apply to Coleridge is, it would seem, the essential issue among those critics discussed in Ch. 2, notes 22, 23, and 25.

usual imaginative insights and powers, are set apart from other men. They may live in proud but tragic isolation, like one of Byron's heroes, or they may, like Hegel's world-historical figures, become leaders of men, the chosen instruments of the World Spirit at work in history. Or they may be one of Carlyle's prophets, teachers, kings, or gods.[10] Thus the doctrine of Reason had its undemocratic consequences, but they were not inevitable. Reason may, as Herder believed, dwell in the great body of common people—to use Rousseau's phrase, in the general will. Instead of the hero it may be the voice of the people that is the voice of God. Thus Romanticism could be either authoritarian or democratic.

Another major characteristic of Romantic thought was an appreciation of the importance of time. Time was less significant in the world-view of the Enlightenment, which saw Nature as a wondrous machine governed by immutable laws. For the Romantics life was synonymous with change; Nature was not a machine but a living organism, never still, always in the process of becoming something different. Since the Romantics believed that the universe itself is forever changing, they sought the principles that governed growth—what Coleridge and Hegel called "Ideas."

This view of Nature was inevitably reflected in other fields. The Enlightenment has been called an unhistorical age, not because it was uninterested in history, but because it tended to see every age as more or less like every other, and devoted its attention to discovering those universal laws that always govern human nature. As we noted above, the Romantic historian tended to divide the past into distinct cultures, each to be assessed according to its own particular standards. When the Romantic looked for more general coherence, he sought the principles that seemed to govern the transition from one age to the next. The Romantic hoped to find order in Nature and history not from the discovery of unchanging universal laws, but from the unmasking of an inherent purpose, goal, or "Idea" in all events, an Idea that would

10. See Carlyle's *Heroes and Hero-worship* (London, 1841). The later development of the Romantic doctrine of the hero is discussed in Eric Bentley, *A Century of Hero-worship* (Philadelphia, Lippincott, 1944).

gradually manifest itself through time.[11] Thus time was an indispensable dimension of truth. The tendency is clearly illustrated in Coleridge's "Idea of the British Constitution."

The emphasis on time and process had many political and social consequences. In general, Romanticism can be said to have promoted a belief in gradual evolution rather than sudden catastrophic change. This tendency, particularly after the French Revolution, was adapted by conservatives to justify their disposition to tolerate imperfection in human affairs and their preference for programs offering gradual improvement rather than sudden apocalyptic change. The evolutionary emphasis of Romanticism, however, was generally adaptable to the requirements of liberal Utopians as well. The perfected society can be achieved for the present even if it is inevitable that present perfection will someday be outmoded. Many of the earlier Romantics were avid partisans of the Revolution—at least in its initial stages. Later Romanticism, in this as in so many of its other traits, appealed to both left and right.[12]

It is significant that nearly all philosophers influenced by Romanticism found it necessary to develop a new evolutionary logic, a logic of process. Hegel's "dialectic" of thesis, antithesis, and

11. See Ch. 2, p. 35, Ch. 5, passim, and Coleridge, *Church and State*, Ch. 1.

12. There has long been a tendency among literary critics to tie Romanticism to the French Revolution. The early Romantic vision of the indwelling divine, an insight so important to the poetic creativity of writers like Blake, Coleridge, and Wordsworth, often corresponded with enthusiasm for the new world that was to be created by the Revolution. And with political disillusionment came poetic dejection. The same pattern existed among numerous Germans. The "dejected" Coleridge became a political conservative and a philosopher. Did he cease to be a Romantic? The answer depends, of course, upon whether there was a profound change in the nature of his ideas. Coleridge recognized no such discontinuity and took pains to show that even in his political thought he had not altered his fundamental principles, but only applied them with greater perception and prudence. See *The Friend*, First Section, Ch. 6 and 16. Whether the later Coleridge should be called Romantic is a question of utility. As this chapter indicates, I find it more useful to stress the continuity between the early and later careers of the at least sometime Romantics.

synthesis was only the most celebrated of the new logics.[13] It was only natural for the Romantic emphasis on process and time to combine with the belief in an immanent divine energy to produce a fatalistic philosophy of history. The progress of the World Spirit is inevitable. Success justifies itself. Coleridge, in his political writings, resisted this tendency and stressed instead the possibility of failure and the necessity for intelligent leadership.[14] This position involved him in numerous logical difficulties, as the previous chapter indicated.

A fascination for the idea of the infinite is another characteristic of many Romantics, and is closely connected with their dynamic view of the universe and their interest in time. For the Romantic as for the Christian, history was progressing somewhere. But the Romantic philosophy of history, unlike the Augustinian, had no predictable last act. *Kraft*, Being, the World Spirit could be seen at work in the past—it can even be experi-

13. Coleridge himself developed an elaborate dialectical logic. See Alice D. Snyder, ed., *Coleridge on Logic and Learning* (New Haven, 1929) and *S. T. Coleridge's Treatise on Method* (London, 1934). See also a recent article by Craig W. Miller, "Coleridge's Concept of Nature," *Journal of the History of Ideas*, 25, (1964), 77–96.

14. It is my contention throughout that although the tensions between faith and rational Reason, determinism and free will, and universals and particulars most assuredly exist in Coleridge's thought as a whole, in his political writings especially, he emphasizes the importance of rationality, choice, and particular circumstances—and hence the possibility of failure and evil in the life of individuals and nations. It is interesting to note that in the "Prospectus" for his lectures on the history of philosophy, Coleridge considered the development of human thought "as if it were the striving of a single mind, under very different circumstances indeed, and at different periods of its own growth and development; but so that each change and every new direction should have its cause and its explanation in the errors, insufficiency, or prematurity of the preceding." (p. 67). Later on, in Lecture II, he was struck by the opposite but yet so complementary characters of Greek and Hebrew civilizations—"imperfect halves which, after a series of ages, each maturing and perfecting, are at length to meet in some one point comprising the excellencies of both" (p. 87)—an observation, he admitted, that came naturally to a mind, presumably such as his own, which "is beforehand impressed with a belief of a providence guiding this great drama of the world to its conclusion." Kathleen Coburn, ed., *The Philosophical Lectures of Samuel Taylor Coleridge* (London, 1949), pp. 67, 87. But for Coleridge, as for Milton in *Paradise Lost*, a providential design in history did not rule out natural law or individual choice, failure, or responsibility.

enced intuitively in the present—but it is forever restless and elusive, forever marching forward to goals beyond the grasp of even the most gifted imagination. The divine energy is infinite or limitless in two senses. It is not bound to any foreseeable conclusion, nor is it fettered by any permanent forms or rules. Each manifestation of the World Spirit—a national culture, for example—postulates its own unique order. As the World Spirit moves on to a new, more modern culture, new science and morality are the inevitable results. The consequent view was a world animated by an infinite and unpredictable vitality.

This view had profound effects upon the mood of the Romantics, and indeed upon that of the entire nineteenth century. The manifestations run from the ceaseless yearning for love that can never be fulfilled to the insatiable desire for imperialist expansion. Cecil Rhodes once confessed that if there were no more Africa he would strive to annex the stars. The motto for the century might be taken from Tennyson's *Ulysses:* "To strive, to seek, to find, and not to yield." It might be added unpoetically, "and never to be satisfied."

While as artists the Romantics favored individualism, in their social and political thought they frequently placed far greater emphasis upon groups than upon single individuals. In this as in many other aspects of their thought they reversed exactly the general tendency of the Enlightenment. The political thinkers who preceded the Romantics—Hobbes, Locke, the *philosophes* —leaned toward an atomistic view of society and the State, with individuals on one side and government on the other. Both were held in their places by enlightened self-interest, mobilized by either absolutist or representative institutions. The Romantic, on the other hand, tended toward an organic rather than an atomistic and mechanical view of society. Politics was seen chiefly as an affair of groups—big all-inclusive groups like the *Volk* or more particular corporate associations within a national society. To Burke, for example, the State was a sacred partnership of the constituent social elements of the nation, held together within a traditional constitutional framework not only by common economic interests, but by loyalties, memories, and identities deeply rooted in the national consciousness. Romantics tended to be appreciative of the nonrational factors involved in politics. Perhaps because of their passionate defense of artistic individuality, they were intensely concerned with the psychological relationship of the individual to the group. Their psychological studies were notable not only for their interest in the irrational and emotional, but for their concern with the problem of the "self" and its identity.[15] Some writers sought by a psychology of identity to reconcile individualism with corporatism—in much the same way perhaps as others sought by the doctrine of Reason to reconcile their appreciation of the irrational with their search for coherence.

The reader must be willing by now to agree with the distinguished scholar, mentioned earlier, who finds the term Romanticism utterly useless. Individualism, irrationalism, historicism, fatalism, corporatism, yearning for the infinite—these are an extraordinarily diverse group of attitudes to bind into a single world-view. What possible justification is there for using a single term to embrace so many opposing tendencies? There would surely be none if it were not that so many great minds of the age—Herder, Schelling, Hegel, and Coleridge—incorporated these traits into their various philosophical systems. In so doing they demonstrated another Romantic trait: a strong faith in the unity of all knowledge. The Enlightenment of course was no less an encyclopedic age. But the Romantics criticized the Enlightenment for attaining a coherent view of reality only by suppressing whole dimensions of human experience. Romantics were determined not to ignore anything that man knows and feels. They believed that a true philosophy could show a deeper coherence behind all the various contrasting forms of human knowledge not by declaring one to be true and the other illusory, but by seeing the higher truth that incorporated both. It was characteristic Romantic doctrine that a truth always contains its opposite. Hegel, the greatest of the Romantic synthesizers, took the logic of opposites and spread it out over history. Through all the confusion and tragedy of man's past, Hegel saw the World Spirit pro-

15. The Romantic ego is dealt with at length in Lovejoy, *The Reason*, and Barzun, *Classic, Romantic, and Modern*. An interesting development of the Romantic psychology of the self can be found in the British neo-Hegelian philosopher, Bernard Bosanquet, *The Psychology of the Moral Self* (London and New York, 1897).

ceeding by apparent opposites to the development of higher and higher forms of human society. Only the great historian could perceive "the cunning of Reason," but it was nevertheless at work. There was purpose and coherence in history as in all knowledge. The double concern for comprehensiveness and coherence produced, in the great Romantic thinkers, philosophical systems remarkable for their scope and erudition, perhaps wearisome in the complexity of their details yet majestic in their powerful straining toward ultimate coherence.

Of course not all figures of the Romantic age achieved or even sought such a reconciliation of opposing traits. Nor were they willing to accept the positions of those who did. Most exhibited some traits labeled Romantic but not others. Romantics were no less divided than medieval Christians, and they lacked a Church to mediate, dogmatize, or even give them a sense of common purpose and identity. Nor was it uncommon for Romantics to cease being "Romantic," to lose their faith and hence their Reason. The difficulty with World Spirits and similar devices is that they must be believed to be seen.

As one would expect, it has been possible for critics to perceive certain stages in the development of Romanticism. At first, the Romanticism of *Sturm und Drang*, can be seen as primarily concerned with freedom from the Enlightenment. It was a disorderly and emotional Romanticism, mainly destructive and negative. Politically and socially, this phase tended to be radical and indeed revolutionary. Most Romantics greeted the Revolution with great enthusiasm. The second phase was philosophically a positive one and saw the creation of the great Romantic syntheses, the period of Hegel in Germany and Coleridge in England—"High Romanticism." Politically it was more conservative. This reflected not only widespread disillusion with the Revolution, but the inherent Romantic emphasis on time and process rather than sudden catastrophic change. The third stage was disintegration or specialization.[16] The Romantic balance was too precarious and too

16. Jacques Barzun combines the first two stages, dates them from 1780 to 1850, and describes his first stage as "one of extraordinary, unremitting, 'unspecialized' production in all fields." He describes three other stages representing "selection, refinement, and intensification": Realism (roughly 1850–85); Symbolism—also called Impressionism; and Naturalism (both

intellectually arduous to last. The whole movement burst. Its elements spread into the cultural life of the century and gave rise to numerous particular and often conflicting artistic and philosophical schools. Thus Realism, Naturalism, Heroic Vitalism, Symbolism, Darwinism, Wagnerism, and numerous other phenomena can be seen as specialized or bastardized forms of Romanticism.

I hope to suggest and illustrate in this study of Coleridge that the Romantic world-view was extraordinarily suited to perceiving and solving the problems of the modern constitutional State. Preoccupation with the reconciliation of individuality with order, the particular with the general, and the self with the group made the Romantic especially sensitive to the problem of political consensus. Emphasis upon time and development was well adapted to an age that witnessed constant change and needed to be continually adaptable while maintaining a sense of continuity with enduring loyalties and values.

In short, Coleridge's theory of the State is a typical product of Romanticism,[17] as typical as *Kubla Khan*, the paintings of Caspar David Friedrich, or the *Ninth Symphony*. *Church and State* is of a piece not only with the rest of Coleridge's thought, but with the dominant intellectual and spiritual current of his time.

---

roughly 1875–1905). (Barzun, *Classic, Romantic, and Modern*, p. 99.) In a study of Coleridge it seems useful to subdivide Barzun's first category rather than to spell out the varieties of later specialization. It might be noted, however, that many of the great Romantic "synthesizers" first passed through a stage of *Sturm und Drang*, Herder being the most obvious example.

17. Coleridge used the word Romantic in his tenth Philosophical Lecture (March 1, 1819) to describe the inward, imaginative "genius" of the Gothic mind. Miss Coburn notes that the use at this time is more German than English and suggests its relationship to Schiller and Schlegel. Coburn, *The Philosophical Lectures*, pp. 290 and 442. It is interesting that at the beginning of the same lecture Coleridge contrasted the "federal character" of the Goths with the "direct republicanism or the character of a state" typical of Greek politics and of the classic mind in general. The Goths were "belinked together, but no part would lose its own integrity and individuality" (p. 289). Christianity, the Schoolmen, labored to create a synthesis.

CHAPTER 4

Human Nature and Political Theory

When Coleridge applied his method to politics, and above all when he applied his distinction between Reason and the Understanding, it quickly proved to him the fallacies of contemporary Utopians and reactionaries alike. Each held but a partial view of human nature that placed too great an emphasis on one or another of man's faculties to the exclusion of the others. As Coleridge saw it, human nature encompasses three distinct faculties that must be taken into account: Sense, Understanding, and Reason. To begin with, man is a creature of Sense. He possesses pure material needs and animal passions. But man is not simply an animal, but a rational animal, a creature endowed with Understanding, the ability to order his life according to general principles and expectations. And finally, for Coleridge, man is still more. With his Reason, he is something of an angel, perceiving and participating in the divine order that is embodied in the universe. Man is a rational animal with occasional angelic tendencies. He is all these things, but all of them together. Political theory goes astray, Coleridge believed, when it focuses too exclusively on one of these aspects of human nature.

The Utopians made States for angels, the reactionaries for beasts. One would base government on pure Reason alone, the other on coercion and intimidation. Coleridge, defender of the traditional English constitution, sought to discredit both.

It was never as easy for Coleridge to reject the Utopianism of the Revolution as most English conservatives believed it should have been. There was always an ambivalence in his attitude toward the Revolution. Doubtless he was right to assert that he

63

was never a Jacobin, but it is nevertheless true that the young Coleridge was deeply possessed by the reforming zeal and Utopian tendencies of his age. What makes him so interesting later, as a conservative, is that he never lost his reformer's zeal nor his penchant for governing practice by principle. He sought instead to refine and enlarge his principles in accordance with his own growing vision of human nature. To be useful, principles must reflect reality, and neither man nor his world is governed solely by Reason. Pure Reason moves in the realm of pure Ideas, and such Ideas are always universal. The Utopian must invariably postulate a universal ideal: "one constitution and one system of legislation."[1] In this view, anything beyond the uniform and universal rational laws of politics is a superfluous corruption of ideal truth. "Whatever is not everywhere necessary, is nowhere right. On this assumption the whole theory is built."[2] Such reasoning, Coleridge believed, is not political theory, but "metapolitics." Metapolitics might be harmless enough if it were merely the amiable indulgence of recluse philosophers. But as the Revolution made abundantly clear, nothing is more ferociously destructive than the Utopian vision when combined with religious fanaticism and despotic temperament.

Coleridge divided the political Utopians into two schools. There were the democratic followers of such writers as Rousseau, Paine, and Cartwright, and there were the Physiocrats—French partisans of an enlightened despotism. The two groups divided primarily over the question of who was the infallible agent of pure Reason. Rousseau saw the voice of Reason issuing from the assembled people. The Physiocrats, on the contrary, saw Reason coming from the lips of an enlightened despot—properly educated and advised by his council of *philosophes*. Although the Physiocrats were despotic where Rousseau was democratic, both shared, Coleridge believed, a common way of looking at politics. Both based politics upon abstractions derived rationalistically from the postulates of pure Reason. Both were enchanted by the simple clarity of abstract ideals. Both escaped from the complexities of life into the naïve dream world of metapolitics.

Coleridge devoted his most serious attention to Rousseau. Ac-

1. Coleridge, "The Friend," *Works*, 2, 165.
2. Ibid.

cording to Coleridge, Rousseau based his entire political system upon "the freedom, which is the common right of all men, under the control of that moral necessity, which is the common duty of all men."[3] Coleridge agreed that all men share the right to freedom and the corresponding obligation to duty, but he denied Rousseau's subsequent conclusion that all men should share equally in the sovereign power, in the declaring of the general will.

In the first place, Coleridge denied that the people as a whole can be relied upon to perceive and follow the rational general will. Rousseau's general will is clearly not the voice of anyone in particular, but is by definition the pure law of Reason and hence, Coleridge argued, "like the voice of an external ventriloquist . . . indifferent from whose lips it appears to come."[4] To postulate a political theory that is dependent on this voice of Reason emanating from a legislative assembly of all the people is to base the system not upon "a demonstrable deduction from reason," but "a mere probability, against which other probabilities may be weighed."[5] Rousseau himself perceived this possible lack of correspondence and hence made his famous distinction between the "will of all" and the "general will." Coleridge observed:

> all which is said in the *Contrat Social* of that sovereign will, to which the right of universal legislation appertains, applies to no one human being, to no society or assemblage of human beings, and least of all to the mixed multitude that makes up the people: but entirely and exclusively to reason itself, which, it is true, dwells in every man potentially, but actually and in perfect purity is found in no man and in no body of men. This distinction the latter disciples of Rousseau chose completely to forget, and,—a far more melancholy case—the constituent legislators of France forgot it likewise. With a wretched parrotry they wrote and harangued without ceasing of the *volonté général*—the inalienable sovereignty of the people: and by these high-sounding phrases led on the vain, ignorant, and intoxicated populace to wild excesses and wilder expectations, which

3. Ibid.
4. Ibid., p. 178.
5. Ibid.

entailing on them the bitterness of disappointment cleared the way for military despotism, for the Satanic government of horror under the Jacobins, and of terror under the Corsican.[6]

Not only did Coleridge reject the belief that the will of the people is the most reliable expression of pure Reason, but he denied the very relevance of pure Reason and morality to politics. He accused Rousseau of trying to turn the State into a Church, of confusing political prudence with religious morality. Morality is properly concerned not with results, but with intentions. Every man can indeed judge his own motives in the rational light of the Golden Rule:

> But when we pass out of ourselves, and speak, not exclusively of the agent as meaning well or ill, but of the action in its consequences, then of course experience is required, judgment in making use of it, and all those other qualities of the mind which are so differently dispensed to different persons, both by nature and education.[7]

In politics, Coleridge argued, it is not enough to be merely good. One must be wise as well. Political wisdom is not derived primarily from pure Reason, but through the Understanding:

> And though the reason itself is the same in all men, yet the means of exercising it, and the materials,—that is, the facts and conceptions—on which it is exercised, being possessed in very different degrees by different persons, the practical result is, of course, equally different—and the whole ground-work of Rousseau's philosophy ends in a mere nothingism.[8]

This finally is what Coleridge meant when he asserted, in opposition to Rousseau, that politics is a matter for prudence, not pure logic, for the Understanding and not Reason:

> That reason should be our guide and governor is an undeniable truth, and all our notion of right and wrong is built

6. Ibid., p. 179.
7. Ibid., p. 148.
8. Ibid.

thereon: for reason is one of the two fountain-heads in which the whole moral nature of man originated and subsists. From reason alone we derive the principles which our understandings are to apply, the ideal to which by means of our understandings we should endeavor to approximate. This, however, gives no proof that reason alone ought to govern and direct human beings, either as individuals or as states. It ought not to do this, because it can not.[9]

Nothing makes the insufficiency of pure Reason more apparent than a moment's reflection upon the chief concerns and purposes of government. Coleridge saw governments coming into being in the first instance for the preservation of institutions quite irrelevant to pure Reason, chiefly property. However the scope of the State may expand into moral and intellectual spheres, the preservation of the laws of property remains its earliest and most enduring concern. Yet:

> it is impossible to deduce the right of property from pure reason . . . We regard angels and glorified spirits as beings of pure reason: and who ever thought of property in heaven? . . .

Rousseau himself expressly admits that property can not be deduced from the laws of reason and nature . . . his system . . . [is] analogous to geometry . . . Geometry holds forth an ideal which can never be fully realized in nature, even because it is nature; because bodies are more than extension, and to pure extension of space only the mathematical theorems wholly correspond. In the same manner the moral laws of the intellectual world, as far as they are deducible from pure intellect, are never perfectly applicable to our mixed and sensitive nature, because man is something besides reason; because his reason never acts by itself, but must clothe itself in the substance of individual understanding and specific inclination, in order to become a reality and an object of consciousness and experience.[10]

9. Ibid., p. 184.
10. Ibid., pp. 185–86.

In consequence:

> expedience founded on experience and particular circumstances, which will vary in every different nation, and in the same nation at different times . . . [is] the maxim of all legislation and the ground of all legislative power. For his universal principles, as far as they are principles and universal, necessarily suppose uniform and perfect subjects, which are to be found in the ideas of pure geometry and, I trust, in the realities of heaven, but never, never, in creatures of flesh and blood.[11]

Nowhere is the relationship between Coleridge's general philosophy and his political theory more apparent. Coleridge accused Rousseau of placing man in a rational world of tidy universals and forgetting that all creation, including man himself, is a mingling of the universal and the particular, the rational and the irrational. According to Coleridge, nations and men are individuals who can never be governed by uniform and unchanging sets of arrangements based upon the invariable laws of pure Reason and morality. The State is not a Church. Politics is the art of the possible, and its study, like the study of anything else, requires a proper method.

It does credit to Coleridge's critical judgment that he recognized how close he was in many respects to Rousseau's political philosophy, if not his program. Rousseau, particularly as Coleridge interpreted him, asserted so much of what Coleridge once had hoped would be true. To the young poet who found God in himself and everywhere in Nature, to the Coleridge, we might say, of the Primary Imagination, it was not such an absurd and ignoble proposition that God dwelt in the mass of an uncorrupted people. By the time Coleridge had grown older, both he and the world in general were a good deal wiser. But the mature Coleridge had lost more than his political optimism. With it had vanished his spontaneous and effortless vision of divine purpose in all things, and he was left dejected and empty. In his tormented isolation he pressed on with the arduous task of repossessing his vision through the disciplined insights of philosophical knowledge. In-

11. Ibid., p. 187.

evitably he came to place more and more emphasis upon the need for an active and disciplined mind to shape, perfect, and apply the raw truths of intuition. He became the Coleridge of the Secondary Imagination, of aristocracy rather than of democracy. All the same, Coleridge felt that Rousseau professed a noble and generous illusion. Men are not angels, earth is not heaven, but what a pity!

There was no ambivalence, however, in Coleridge's attitude toward the reactionary conservatives of his own country. Few men loved or understood traditional English constitutionalism better than Coleridge. But his devotion only increased his antagonism to the governments of the time. For he saw the greatest danger to traditional England coming not necessarily from its avowed opponents, the Revolutionaries, but from its false defenders, the Tory reactionaries. Before English conservatism could be saved from its foreign enemies, he felt, it must first be rescued from its domestic friends and their contemptible theories.

To begin with, Coleridge had little personal respect for the leading Tory politicians of his day. Long after he had come to abominate the French, he continued to be savagely critical of the Tory ministries of Pitt and Addington. Indeed his greatest journalistic triumph was a devastating analysis of the character of Pitt published in the *Morning Post* on March 19, 1800. Coleridge calls Pitt a frozen child prodigy: "His father's rank, fame, political connections, and parental ambition were his mould;—he was cast, rather than grew."[12] Pitt did not live in the real world of men, Coleridge wrote, but in a private world of cold, bloodless words. Trained from his earliest years to declaim before distinguished audiences, his education consisted always in learning the management of words, never in comprehending the nature of real things. Thus he lacked any insight into the warm and turbulent stream of human events. But "an education of words, though it destroys genius, will often create, and always foster, talent."[13] Young Pitt did acquire a great dexterity of expression and a dazzling facility for dealing with abstractions. This talent, his great connections, and the accidents of history all contrived

12. Sara Coleridge, ed., *Coleridge's Essays on His Own Times* (3 vols. London, Pickering, 1850), 2, 320.

13. Ibid., p. 321.

to make him, at twenty-five, the leader of his country. What sort of man was he, Coleridge asks:

—A plant sown and reared in a hot-house, for whom the very air that surrounded him, had been regulated by the thermometer of previous purpose; to whom the light of nature had penetrated only through glasses and covers; who had had the sun without the breeze; whom no storm had shaken; on whom no rain had pattered; on whom the dews of heaven had not fallen!—A being, who had had no feelings connected with man or nature, no spontaneous impulses, no unbiassed and desultory studies, no genuine science, nothing that constitutes individuality in intellect, nothing that teaches brotherhood in affection! Such was the man—such, and so denaturalised the spirit, on whose wisdom and philanthropy the lives and living enjoyments of so many millions of human beings were made unavoidably dependent.[14]

For Addington, Coleridge expressed unrelieved contempt:

We have already hinted our opinions of the abilities of Mr. ADDINGTON. They are beneath mediocrity . . .

Mr. PITT puzzles his audience by his ingenuity, Mr. ADDINGTON by his confusion. The one renders himself unintelligible by his sophistry; the other is not understood, because that which is not clearly conceived, can never be clearly and definitely expressed. He never displays dexterity in debate, expansion or vigour of mind, a strong discriminating power, originality of thought, or richness of fancy. His intellect is too short-sighted to see beyond the point immediately before him, and hence, in a case of complexity, it is mere chance if one part of his argument does not contradict the other. He is easily thrown into confusion, and he betrays a total want of ability to rally. He cannot repair an error, or cover a retreat. Whenever he is defeated, the defeat is most decisive. There is scarcely a public occasion in which

14. Ibid., p. 323.

his powers have been brought into action, that does not furnish proof of these remarks.[15]

Several years later, in *The Friend*, Coleridge reflected upon the sins of English conservatives during the revolutionary era. Their chief crime in his view was an hysterical reliance upon violence in both argument and action. They succeeded in whipping themselves into a "panic of property," and in their self-induced frenzy were convinced that they lived, surrounded by a diabolical conspiracy, in a country ripe for revolution. By behaving this way they threw away all the natural advantages of their position. They abandoned their own traditional constitutionalism to embrace the very kind of domestic despotism the English had always so gloriously resisted. They became as callous about trampling over laws, rights, and traditions as the Revolutionaries, and thus they themselves became enemies of stability. They made no effort to win over the minds of their opponents or to welcome those whose views had changed. They came more and more in the grip of a great fear and were satisfied only by harsh and heavy-handed displays of coercive force.

The Tories had developed this disgusting predilection for coercion, Coleridge said, because they had adopted a way of looking at human nature and politics that was no less false than that of the Utopians and infinitely less attractive. Whereas the Utopians saw man as a creature guided by Reason, the Tories saw him motivated primarily by "Sense." While for Rousseau man was an angel, for the reactionaries he was a beast. Both views were absurdly one-sided. Neither saw man for what he is—a creature endowed with an Understanding that must mediate the demands of the differing sides of his complex nature.

For Coleridge, Hobbes was the classic example of a theorist who focused too exclusively upon Sense as an element in human psychology and who, in consequence, was led to the conclusion that coercion was the single essential and inevitable element of a political system. Hobbes' view of human nature, according to Coleridge, reduces man to a cunning and selfish animal with insatiable material desires. Accordingly Hobbes taught that peace

15. *Morning Post*, March 22, 1802, as reproduced in John Colmer, *Coleridge: Critic of Society* (Oxford, 1959), pp. 216–17.

can only come to human society by the imposition of a single will with the irresistible power to coerce men into political order. Force is the basis of the State. Coleridge regarded this theory as so absurd that "Its statement is its confutation."[16]

Of course Coleridge disagreed with Hobbes on almost every point of philosophy, ethics, and psychology. Whereas in Coleridge's view Rousseau would base the State upon those universal ethical norms available to all men through their Reason, Hobbes denied that men shared any such norms except the instinct of self-preservation. Rousseau dwelt in the midst of harmonious universals, Hobbes in a disordered world of quarreling particulars. Hobbes in effect denied the existence of Reason, as Coleridge defined it. Man possesses a rational calculating faculty, the Understanding; it is presented with its goals not by semi-divine Reason, but by animal Sense. Hobbes was doubtless right in concluding that if his view of man was correct there was no basis for order in human affairs except imposed force, for the cravings of Sense are insatiable and hence lead inevitably to the war of all against all.

Coleridge devoted little space to refuting Hobbes on a philosophical level. He focused his criticism rather upon the empirical inadequacy of Hobbesian psychology. If man were as Hobbes found him, government of any kind would be impossible. Hobbes was not only ignoble, but impractical. Man cannot be ruled by fear alone:

> We are told by history, we learn from our experience, we know from our own hearts, that fear, of itself, is utterly incapable of producing any regular, continuous, and calculable effect, even on an individual; and that the fear, which does act systematically upon the mind, always pre-supposes a sense of duty, as its cause.[17]

> Hobbes has said, that laws without the sword are but bits of parchment. How far this is true, every honest man's heart will best tell him, if he will content himself with asking his own heart, and not falsify the answer by his notions concerning the hearts of other men. But were it true, still the

16. Coleridge, "The Friend," *Works*, 2, 154.
17. Ibid., p. 155.

fair answer would be—Well! but without the laws the sword is but a piece of iron.[18]

In short, the Hobbesian view of human nature is patently inadequate to explain the realities of political behavior. The moral instinct of man, the feeling of duty and loyalty, is an element indispensable to society. Political theory must be written for men, not beasts. While every government does occasionally need force to coerce the unruly, where, Coleridge asked, is the force to come from if not from the allegiance of loyal citizens? That military force without popular support evaporates was the pointed lesson of the French Revolution. Inevitably, as Hume noted, a regime must derive its authority and power from the sense of loyalty it inspires among its subjects. For Coleridge, Hobbes' coercive definition of the State could not explain political allegiance. Coleridge turned, like Rousseau and Burke, to an entirely different approach to defining the State. He saw the State not as a government coercing subjects, but as a great partnership of all the citizens, a tacit social contract between each citizen and all.

Coleridge's criticism of Hobbes was at best rather crude. It is not true, of course, that Hobbes based his State on force alone. Coleridge, however, was less opposed to Hobbes particularly than he was to the whole legalistic tradition of defining the State as coercion. This was the great tradition springing from Augustine, reformulated by Hobbes, and repeated by such nineteenth-century legalists as Bentham and Austin. They saw the State essentially as a band of governors, a specific group within society charged with the special function of maintaining law and order. What distinguishes this group from all others in society is its possession of sovereignty—defined as the final authority to make rules—and it can be said to possess this "sovereign" authority only when it has a monopoly of physical coercion. The monopoly of force is the critical factor in defining the State. Where this monopoly did not exist, as for example in some periods of the Middle Ages, it can be argued that no State existed. Wherever in this tradition the social contract is made use of, it is a contract between a government and its subjects whereby the latter agree to bind themselves to a sovereign in return for peace.

18. Ibid., p. 160.

For Coleridge, this approach to politics was at worst dangerous and at best useless. It was dangerous because it reinforced the stupid Tory predilection for heavy-handed repression. It was useless because it contributed nothing to an understanding of the factors that create stable political allegiance. In the age of the French Revolution, with all classes increasingly aroused politically, consensus was the chief practical and theoretical challenge of the day. If conservatives were to preserve what was best in the traditional order, they had to find some means to capture the lost allegiance of the disaffected elements of society. The fall of the *ancien régime,* the Revolution, and the Napoleonic aftermath all seemed to demonstrate that Hobbes was wrong, that force alone could not create consensus.

What could? Like Rousseau, Coleridge focused on analyzing the factors that maintain political loyalty and legitimacy. Like Rousseau, he turned to another, the "Idealist," tradition of defining the State, which originated in Plato and Aristotle, strongly influenced medieval writers, was introduced into the modern world by Rousseau, and was greatly elaborated on by Hegel and the British Idealists. This tradition emphasized cooperation rather than coercion. The State is viewed not as a special group of governors within the society, but as an association congruent with the whole society. The citizens contract with each other to form a body-politic—a collective moral person capable of acting as a single individual with a single will and binding each of the members. Whereas the essential characteristic of the State in the former tradition is its ability to coerce the unruly, in the latter the essential characteristic is the ability to maintain the bonds of loyalty that unite the citizens in a cooperative partnership. It is not difficult to see why this latter Idealist tradition was not only more appealing to Coleridge, but more useful.

The most valuable modern contribution to the theory of the State has been in the field of psychology. During the nineteenth century and since, the relationship between the self and the group has been explored with unequaled thoroughness and imagination. This development certainly owed its beginning to Romanticism. With their interest in the emotions, the Romantics emancipated the study of the human mind from the narrow mechanistic psychology of Hobbes and Locke. Political theory could then proceed to develop an adequate psychology of consensus and hence a richer view of the State.

As poet and critic, Coleridge ranks as one of the greatest Romantic students of the mind. His psychological insights are reflected in his whole view of the State and its constitution. The explicit connection between his advanced psychological speculations and his political theory is found not so much in his published writings as in the Notebooks. They reveal explicitly, if haphazardly, the psychological dimension of his theory of the State. They show him to have anticipated a psychology of political identity not formally developed in England until half a century later. When Coleridge finally turned from criticizing partial views and undertook the task of creating his own grand theory of the State, that theory was as much informed by his psychological notions about identity as by his philosophical distinction between Reason and Understanding. Both combined to produce an analysis of the British constitution remarkable both for its comprehensiveness and for its detail.

CHAPTER 5

The Psychological Basis of the State

Coleridge's treatise on the State, the *Constitution of Church and State According to the Idea of Each*, was not published until late in his life. It is his greatest political work. The most significant word in the title is "Idea," a notion he used to bind together the three distinct but closely related principles that inform his whole view of the State:

1. The essence of a State is psychological; the State exists primarily as an Idea in the minds of its citizens.
2. The institutional structure or "Constitution" of a State reflects the Idea of that Constitution, held in the minds of the citizens from one generation to the next.
3. The Idea of the Constitution is a particular reflection, within a distinctive national tradition, of an ideal universal Constitution arising out of human nature.

The first two principles are empirical analytical concepts derived from Coleridge's studies in political psychology and English history. The third is essentially philosophical, and reflects his basic view of a universe that is dynamic but orderly, governed by scientific and ethical laws. Thus Coleridge's Idea combines psychological, historical, and philosophical elements. For the purpose of analysis, these dimensions must be treated separately. But it should not be forgotten that they are ultimately complementary, and that Coleridge's theory of the State cannot be understood properly unless they are seen in their integral relation to each other.

Coleridge began by making a distinction between two proper uses of the word State. His distinction parallels the two traditional ways of defining the political community. In Coleridge the word State can refer to the actual political institutions by which a nation is governed—King in Parliament. Or it can refer to the entire national community—the partnership of all citizens and all national institutions, including what Coleridge called the National Church. The State in the first sense is an element within the State taken in the second sense. *Church and State* is primarily an attempt to define the larger State. When Coleridge tried to condense his whole view into a sentence, he defined the State as "a body politic having the principle of its unity within itself."[1] In this instance condensation did not contribute to clarity. What is meant by "the principle of its unity within itself"? Presumably Coleridge meant several things. First of all, "within itself" implies that a State must be self-sufficient as an association, 'sovereign' in the sense that its existence is not immediately contingent upon some other community. Secondly, Coleridge would agree with Locke that a State, although made up of numerous individuals, must be capable of formulating a single will and thus be able to act as a single body. Otherwise the State lacks a 'principle of unity' and disintegrates.

What is it that holds together such a community and gives it its principle of unity? What is the essence of this consensus? In what is it grounded? What maintains it? To begin with, these are psychological questions. While *Church and State* may be said to reflect Coleridge's advanced psychological theories, it does not set them forth explicitly. His psychological definition of the State is made explicit in the unpublished Notebooks.

A State is essentially not territory or governing institutions, but a partnership of loyal citizens. Men are citizens of a State because they share a common loyalty and identification—a common Idea of the association to which they belong. Strictly speaking the Idea itself is the State: "The State is actual only in the Idea. The Idea is the Reality of the State, yea, *is* the State."[2] Men animated by this Idea form a political nation: "The State is the disembodied yet not bodiless Soul (*anima unifica et integrans*) of

1. Coleridge, "Church and State," *Works*, 6, 37.
2. Coleridge, Notebook 44, fol. 64ʳ.

the Nation—each Generation of the individual Citizens being the Body, organized even to its ultimate fibres, but like all Bodies, subsisting in a perpetual and continual flux of its particles."[3] The State then is a notion existing in the minds of its citizens—a shared Idea which acts as a magnet that brings a coherence into the separate individual particles of the nation and gives the body of citizens something analogous to the self-contained unity or wholeness of a single organism. The State is an Idea possessed by or possessing a determinate body of people. By sharing the Idea, the group becomes a political nation—the objective manifestation of the Idea of the State.

Although his language may be recondite, there is nothing remarkable in Coleridge's view that the State is essentially a psychological idea. The same can be said of any group—or rather of any group that is self-conscious—where the members are aware of themselves as a group. The essence of the group is the Idea shared by its members, and possibly by those who are not members. It is this Idea that really constitutes the group. The group may develop objective institutions. But though a group may be entirely informal and exist without any institutions, no group can exist without an Idea. It is tautological that no group can be self-conscious without having an Idea. Why not admit then Coleridge's "Idealist" contention that the essence of the group is the shared Idea? The failure to perceive that a nation is essentially psychological has resulted in a good deal of wasted time searching for objective criteria that absolutely determine nationality. There are none.

If the State is an Idea, where does that Idea come from—or, more importantly, what maintains the individual's adherence to it? Political theorists have of course found numerous factors that nourish the State in the mind of the individual citizen. Traditionally it has been argued that allegiance is maintained for both economic and moral reasons. Modern writers have tended to add psychological inducements as well. Hume and Talleyrand based allegiance on habit. Rousseau placed great emphasis on ceremony and made a tentative and uncertain step toward a psychology of political identity.

Coleridge employed all these insights. He saw consensus not

3. Notebook 44, fol. 64ᵛ.

as the product of a single element, but of a complex of factors. He agreed with Locke that the first basis of the State is economic—the desire of men to safeguard and increase their property. "The chief object for which men first formed themselves into a state was not the protection of their lives, but of their property."[4] On the other hand, he agreed with Rousseau that property alone is not a sufficient basis for consensus. To begin with, man has aspirations beyond material well-being. He looks to the community to satisfy his intellectual, moral, and psychological needs as well. Furthermore property itself is a major cause of social dissension. Coleridge agreed that class war would destroy freedom unless it was possible to mobilize an allegiance to the common good that would in the final analysis transcend more particular loyalties and interests. And like Rousseau, Coleridge recognized the vital importance of education and ceremony as the means by which this devotion is animated and nourished.

Coleridge employed another argument common among nationalists of his time: "in order to be men we must be patriots."[5] A man without a country is not fully a man. Like Herder, Coleridge believed citizenship is as necessary for the artist and philosopher as for the average person. An independent national State is essential to artistic and philosophical creativity within a national culture. The great geniuses of mankind—Plato, Newton, Luther, and their equals—though their accomplishments belong to all mankind were themselves the products of "a circle defined by human affections . . . where the powers and interests of men spread without confusion through a common sphere . . . Here, and here only, may we confidently expect those mighty minds to be reared and ripened, whose names are naturalized in foreign lands."[6]

The most magnificent culture, Coleridge believed, fades with the loss of national independence. The Greeks furnished the most notable illustration:

> While they were intense patriots, they were the benefactors of all mankind, legislators for the very nation that after-

---

4. Coleridge, "The Friend," *Works,* 2, 184–85.
5. Ibid., p. 269.
6. Ibid., pp. 266–67.

wards subdued and enslaved them. When, therefore, they became pure cosmopolites, and no partial affections interrupted their philanthropy, and when yet they retained their country, their language, and their arts, what noble works, what mighty discoveries may we not expect from them? If the applause of a little city, the first-rate town of a country not much larger than Yorkshire, and the encouragement of a Pericles, produced a Phidias, a Sophocles, and a constellation of other stars scarcely inferior in glory, what will not the applause of the world effect, and the boundless munificence of the world's imperial masters? Alas! no Sophocles appeared, no Phidias was born; individual genius fled with national independence, and the best products were cold and laborious copies of what their fathers had thought and invented in grandeur and majesty. At length nothing remained, but dastardly and cunning slaves, who avenged their own ruin and degradation by assisting to degrade and ruin their conquerors; and the golden harp of their divine language remained only as the frame on which priests and monks spun their dirty cobwebs of sophistry and superstition![7]

When Aristotle declared man a political animal, he was saying much the same thing as the modern cultural nationalist. It remained for the moderns, however, to develop a psychological theory to explain the necessary relation between the self and the State. Coleridge developed the outlines of such a theory in his Notebooks. He speculated at some length on the tendency of the individual to identify his own personality with that of his nation:

> The Subject who kneels in homage before a rightful king, as the Symbol and acknowledged Representative of the Unity of the Nation . . . [recognizes] in the Symbol of the Nation simultaneously an image—of his *very Self* successively[?], becomes a King—and a King *indeed* would in receiving his Homage inwardly perform the same, and repeat it in his own Soul as a homage to the great *Idea*, of which

7. Ibid., p. 269.

Providence had made him the Outward Word, the material Exponent.[8]

This shared identity is what lies behind the royal "We" and the term "Majesty." Thus the royal "We" is properly used only in free states, based upon consent and not force. For the plural–singular implies that the ruler himself is not the State, but merely the exponent of an association of free men. The device was certainly not appropriate to an oriental potentate, who doubtless would have beheaded any one who implied that he was ruler, not as a distinct personage, but only as the highest summary of his miserable people.

Coleridge speculated further about the role of a king. There seems to be, he noted, an ineradicable tendency in republics as in monarchies for one man to become a symbol for the whole State. Coleridge found this phenomenon explained in the psychology of the average citizen. While the citizen is in some degree compelled to sacrifice his individual identity by assuming a larger identity within the State, he nevertheless "craves and seeks for a reproduction of his sensible Individuality"—now "no longer as *his* but that of all."[9] This "all" is the whole body of citizens, the State. But the State is a rather abstract idea and hence tends to be general rather than individual. It is difficult to love generalized abstractions or to identify with them. "The problem is solved in the term Symbol—i.e. an Individual Representative of the Universal." Thus "while we contemplate our integrity in the Idea, i.e. the State, we seek to behold our Individuality in the Symbol—the Sovereign of the State."[10] Hence, Coleridge concluded, a Republic without some Head of State is an unnatural government.

But why should the average citizen be in urgent need of a symbol for his lost individuality? Why is his own self "no longer his . . . but that of all"? Because, Coleridge concluded, it is only through participation within such groups as the State that the individual achieves not only ethical responsibility, but his own personal identity. Man is not given his own identity. It is something

8. Notebook 55, fol. 9ʳ and 9ᵛ.
9. Notebook 44, fol. 64ᵛ.
10. Notebook 44, fol. 65ʳ.

he arrives at by playing a role, by placing himself in relation to other men and things.

Coleridge began a significant early Notebook entry with what seemed an apostrophe to human individuality:

> The individuality of Man, how wonderful. No one merely man, as every Tyger is simply Tyger, little more than numerically distinguishable—but this man, with *these* faculties, *these* tendencies, this peculiar character—his Wishes, Hopes, Actions, Fortunes.[11]

But a few pages later his thought took another turn:

> Could a man conceive himself and another fellow-being existing, with our own faculties and impulses, and all around a chaos of indistinction . . . We know each other's presence . . . e contra, our communion consists in the reciprocal knowledge, in the generation of an I by a Thou.[12]

The very passage we began with concludes:

> [The nature of the individual] appears conditioned and determined by an outward Nature, that comprehends his own—what each individual *bears out*, (Homo Phainomenon) depends, as it seems, on the narrow Circumstances and Inclosure of his Infancy, Childhood, and Youth—and afterwards on the larger Hedge-girdle of the State, in which he is a Citizen born . . . he seems to be influenced and determined and caused to be what he is, qualis sit—qualified, *bethinged* by a Universal Nature, its' elements and relations. Beyond this ring-fence he cannot stray.[13]

But are not these "externals" actually part of his own self, for the notion of the self becomes an empty abstraction when it is separated from all the particulars that shape it:

> the more steadily he contemplates this fact, the more deeply he meditates on these workings, the more clearly it dawns up in him that this conspiration of influences is no mere out-

11. Notebook 3¹/₂, fol. 128ʳ.
12. Notebook 3¹/₂, fol. 143ᵛ.
13. Notebook 3¹/₂, fol. 128ʳ and 128ᵛ.

ward nor contingent Thing, that rather this necessity *is* himself, that that without which or divided from which his Being can not be even *thought* must therefore in all its' directions and labyrinthine folds belong to his Being, and evolves out of his essence. Abstract from these and what remains? A general Term, after all the conceptions, notices, and experiences represented by it, had been removed—an Ens logicum.[14]

Near the end of his life Coleridge wrote:

true Philosophy is that the self is in and by itself a Phantom ... because it is capable of receiving true entity by *reflection* from the *Nation*. It strives to become by the act of radiating to the periphery; and it actually becomes, it *is*, by the reflecting, the reflection of itself from the Periphery—without the resisting and returning outline it would be lost in vague space [?] and be forever a mere striving at Being, a pure Selfness.[15]

Coleridge exhibited a typically Romantic suspicion of abstract universals not only in his opposition to abstract individualism— the self contemplated apart from the elements that "bething" it— but in his aversion to cosmopolitanism. Not only is "self" an empty abstraction, but so is "mankind." A nation is something real to the imagination of the citizen. It is sufficiently particular to have a definite personality of its own. It becomes distinct *"e contra"*—in relation to the personalities of other nations. But mankind, as distinct from nationality, is too abstract to be grasped by the imagination and too empty an ideal to be loved by the great mass of men. The humanitarian impulse toward cosmopolitanism results paradoxically in atomized, selfish individualism. To teach the average man to love mankind instead of his own nation is in effect to teach him to love no one but himself: "I detest the principle of modern Political Economy, as necessarily degrading and *denationalizing*—proceeding from Self as the *real* to an *All*, which is a mere abstraction, an infinite Space."[16]

14. Notebook 3½, fol. 129^r.
15. Notebook 55, fol. 10^r.
16. Notebook 55, fol. 9^v and 10^r.

To Coleridge the cosmopolite is either like the Catholics, attempting to substitute a new State for the existing State, or else partakes in:

> a heartless Hypocrisy, which pretends [?] the love of *all* as a substitute and compensation [?] for the Love of anyone but himself. He loves no one—but thus, to be sure, he loves *all*. It would be more *substantial* if he loved the figures, A L L, or the *sound, All*. For these *are* something, whereas All is a mere abstract term.[17]

While Coleridge's scattered writings on the self and political identification show him to have anticipated a psychology of political association not worked out in England until several decades later, it is well to be cautious in considering his affinity to later psychological theories. As noted earlier, Coleridge's notions about political identity were absorbed into the whole fabric of his formal political philosophy, but his explicit writings on the subject are contained mostly in his Notebooks. They were therefore often expressed not only in a tentative and unfinished form, but also without the counterbalancing checks and cautions he would have felt compelled to include in a formal and more comprehensive statement of his views. It would be erroneous to read into Coleridge's occasional notes on the unreality of the individual apart from his setting the same lack of concern for individualism that has characterized some more recent political theories based on the same psychology. For Coleridge the individual is neither morally nor psychologically dissolved into the State. The self may tend to expand, to embrace things beyond its immediate boundaries. It may even require a role in some larger context before it can be aware of itself, but the self is not willingly imposed upon. The tendency to expand identity is combined with a strong resistance to alien intrusions.

At one point Coleridge sought to gain insight into the fundamental traits of human nature by observing small children. He concluded:

> The first lesson, that innocent childhood affords me, is—that it is an instinct of my Nature to pass out of myself, and to exist in the form of others.

17. Notebook 55, fol. 10^{v}.

The second is—not to suffer any one form to pass into *me* and to become a usurping *Self* in the disguise of what the German Patriologists call a *fixed Idea*.[18]

In short, Coleridge did not try to resolve the tension between individual and State by dissolving the individual. And it would be unfair and inaccurate to take scattered notes out of context as indicative of his balanced views on the nature of political association.

Our present intellectual climate is still so permeated by fear and loathing of totalitarianism that we are unlikely to be insensitive to the dangers inherent in the psychology of identity applied to politics. Of all theories it seems most easily susceptible to grotesque and terrifying perversion. On the other hand, it should not be overlooked just how essential such a psychology is to any adequate theoretical defense of the modern constitutional State. The old associationalist psychology that based the State on self-interest is surely bankrupt for constitutionalist theory. It leads either back to Hobbes or forward to Marx. It envisages consensus based either on a permanent despotic force or on the harmony of interest that can arise only after all diversity is eliminated from society. The constitutionalist could scarcely argue in the nineteenth century that a society made up of diverse classes, each pursuing its own private interests, could somehow achieve an automatic general harmony. What the constitutionalist needed to show was that there was a common loyalty and identity which, if properly nourished, could give rise to a general will or interest to which individual persons and groups would, when necessary, be willing to defer their more private demands. By establishing that every individual did indeed have a public as well as a private self, it was possible to show convincingly how a State could preserve diversity and yet manage to be founded upon cooperation rather than coercion.

It seems difficult to dispute Coleridge's basic Idealist contention that no community based primarily upon coercion rather than cooperative consent can be a good society. A prison can never be a good society no matter how efficiently or humanely it is run. On the other hand, consent is not a sure indication of vir-

18. Notebook 47, fol. 20^{r} and 20^{v}.

tue. Modern totalitarianism is uniquely evil not because it coerces men into barbarism, but because it insists upon, and so often obtains, their enthusiastic consent. But it is foolish to assume that totalitarianism is somehow the inevitable outcome of the cooperative Idealist tradition. We can ill afford to do without the tremendous insights of the Idealist writers merely because some of their ideas, wrenched out of context, have been subjected to grotesque parody. It would surely be more sensible to realize, as Coleridge did, that while consensus is essential to any State that is not to be ruled by brute force, consensus itself is amoral. It is necessary to the good State, but certainly not sufficient. The citizens may be partners in crime as well as in virtue. For Coleridge the totalitarian State would be evil not because it demands the love of its citizens, but because it uses that love to make them inhuman. Whether a cooperative State is good or bad depends upon the content of its consensus.

No one can accuse Coleridge of unconcern with the content of the Idea around which consensus was built in England. Except for a few paragraphs, his entire published writing on the State is concerned with the Idea, not as a psychological concept, but as a specific body of beliefs current throughout English history. For him the Idea that was England was not some shadowy and vague sense of loyalty to the nation, but certain persistent constitutional principles that had, on the whole, succeeded in creating a good society and maintaining it over the centuries. This content, or "Constitution," of the Idea of the State was Coleridge's chief concern.

The Constitution was defined as that actual arrangement of powers, rights, and duties by which the political community was governed and given its coherence—its necessary unity. More specifically, it was the system of understandings and practices by which the elements of English society managed to coexist in union. Logically that unity might result from some single, overwhelming Hobbesian force in the realm. In practice, however, unity was always the result of a durable balance of forces—similar in many ways to the balance maintained between the elements in an organism. This durable balance made up the Constitution of the body-politic. It was the network of habitual relationships, formal and informal, among the groups and institutions of English society.

What distinguishes the Coleridgean Constitution from a simple reckoning of where active power lies from one moment to the next? What makes any particular balance of competing forces durable? Coleridge's whole method provided the answer. For him the Constitution was more than a mere snapshot of a particular and momentary balance of forces. It was more stable because behind it was an Idea, firmly planted in the minds of the English people, an Idea, Coleridge believed, that had animated English politics from the very beginnings of the nation.

Coleridge described at some length how such Ideas influence political behavior. The failure to recognize their influence came chiefly, he argued, from treating Ideas as mere "conceptions." By way of illustration he applied his familiar distinction between conception and Idea to the notion of the Social Contract. As a conception, formed *a posteriori*, the Social Contract is meaningless, as Hume amply demonstrated. There is no historical evidence that the people ever entered into actual contractual agreement, and if they had there is no reason why their descendants should feel morally obliged to honor a merely arbitrary convention.

But, Coleridge argued, if the Social Contract is taken as the Idea that should inform the relationship between citizen and ruler, then it expresses" the whole ground of the difference . . . between a commonwealth and a slave-plantation."[19] For the Social Contract, as an Idea, is simply a shorthand way of expressing the whole notion of government by consent. As an Idea, the Social Contract itself is the political extension of a yet more fundamental Idea, that of "person in contra-distinction to thing."[20] Sheep are bred, sheared, and killed; trees are planted and cut—all means to our ends. "The wood-cutter and the hind are likewise employed as means, but on agreement, and that too an agreement of reciprocal advantage, which includes them as well as their employer in the end; for they are persons."[21] Similarly political au-

19. Coleridge, "Church and State," *Works*, 6, 32.
20. Ibid.
21. Ibid., p. 33.

thority, to be morally valid, requires the consent of the governed.

An Idea of this sort is *a priori* in the sense that its validity and power do not depend upon formal promulgation. The Idea is rooted in the public mind. Laws, conventions, and treatises may articulate or at least reflect the Idea. They do not create it *de novo*, although some particular expressions may have great influence on its later development. The Declaration of Independence did not create the Ideas it contained. Yet that particular expression of them had great influence on their subsequent development.

It is further characteristic of Ideas in politics that they can rarely be expressed as complete or clear propositions even by those who are most inspired by them. Coleridge's friends, the hind and the woodsman, are unlikely to have read Kant or to understand his philosophical distinctions. Nevertheless, Coleridge argued, they know well enough the distinction between man and thing:

> no man, who has ever listened to laborers of this rank, in any alehouse, over the Saturday night's jug of beer, discussing the injustice of the present rate of wages, and the iniquity of their being paid in part out of the parish poor-rates, will doubt for a moment that they are fully possessed by the idea.[22]

For Coleridge the British Constitution is, like the Social Contract, essentially an Idea. More specifically, it is the notion held by Englishmen that the healthy State demands a proper balance of distinctive elements or groups—each carrying on its unique activities and making its own special demands, and yet, if health is to be preserved, each subordinated to the good of the whole.

Although a political philosopher may discuss a constitutional ideal in terms of abstract balances, these balances must always be struck through the unique institutions of each particular time and place. Hence no actual Constitution is at any moment a finished and perfected model. The Idea of the Constitution, then, is not a fixed set of arrangements, but rather a principle regulating change. Coleridge believed that, throughout the development of

22. Ibid.

the particular institutions of England, the subjects of that king-
dom had been animated by certain notions of a just balance:

> our whole history from Alfred onwards demonstrates the
> continued influence of such an idea, or ultimate aim, on the
> minds of our forefathers, in their characters and functions
> as public men, alike in what they resisted and in what they
> claimed; in the institutions and forms of polity which they
> established, and with regard to those, against which they
> more or less successfully contended.[23]

So strong has been the influence of the Idea that even the most
radical, Coleridge noted, have seldom described their demands as
innovations, but rather as a return to better days or the true spirit
of the Constitution. Those who would change things have as frequently invoked the traditional Constitution as have their opponents. Nor were they necessarily wrong to do so, even if their historical scholarship was preposterous. Unconsciously at least, they
appealed not to what the Constitution had ever been, but rather
to what it ought to be if the principles that had informed its
growth in the past were adapted to present circumstances or
carried further toward their logical conclusions. This is what
Coleridge had in mind when he spoke of the Idea as that notion
of something "which is not abstracted from any particular state,
form, or mode, in which the thing may happen to exist at this or
that time; nor yet generalized from any number or succession of
such forms or modes; but which is given by the knowledge of its
ultimate aim."[24] To which we should add, for Coleridge, its "ultimate aim" as perceived at the time.

Many of Coleridge's critics have treated the whole notion of
the Idea as incomprehensible philosophical moonshine. But there
is nothing necessarily occult in such a theory of the Constitution.
Indeed it is difficult to make much sense out of constitutional history without the aid of something like Coleridge's Idea. If, for
example, the American Constitution is viewed as a "conception,"
it is difficult to avoid the conclusion that the present-day Supreme Court is characterized either by extremely bad scholarship
or a cynical disregard for the Constitution. Certainly the Court

23. Ibid., pp. 34–35.
24. Ibid., p. 30.

has developed new doctrines that can scarcely be justified on strictly scholarly grounds, either by original text or intention, or even by later precedent. The only argument that salvages both the Court's integrity and its intelligence is that the American Constitution is essentially an Idea. Like all Ideas it contains principles that must be reinterpreted according to particular circumstances. Furthermore, the Idea contains elements with an inherent dynamism—notions that lead to conclusions that inevitably lead to further conclusions. The Supreme Court is the keeper of the Idea of the Constitution—a role calling for philosophical, historical, and political as well as legal talent.

So far Coleridge's definition of the State has been treated in its empirical aspects. To Coleridge the State is essentially an Idea shared by the citizens and essential to their own identity. Further, the Idea has content. It implies a Constitution—an arrangement of rights and powers believed by the citizens to be the proper character of their State. The introduction of content into the Idea raises two great questions, one practical and the other philosophical, both ethical. It is impossible for all citizens to share precisely the same notions about what is the proper constitution or Idea of their State. It is more than likely that their differences will be considerable and of great importance to them. Who decides? Who is the legitimate keeper or spokesman for the Idea —King, people, Church, or judiciary? The first question leads inevitably to the second. What is the basis for deciding whose opinion is right? In what is the Idea of the Constitution grounded— public opinion, custom, culture, human nature, natural or divine law?

In *Church and State* Coleridge turns directly to the first question. His answer to the second must be gleaned not so much from particular statements as from his entire philosophical system. With respect to the first question, it is always perfectly clear that the Idea is meant to be more than momentary public opinion. As we have already noted, Coleridge made the same distinction as Rousseau between the general will and the will of all. For Coleridge, there is nothing infallible about *vox populi*. It may as easily be *vox diaboli* as *vox dei*. The Idea is meant to be a standard against which present opinions, institutions, and demands are all to be measured—a standard "in the light of which it can alone be ascertained what are excrescences, symptoms of distemperature, and marks of degeneration; and what are native growths, or changes naturally attendant on the progressive development of the original germ."[25] The Supreme Court would be expected to strike down legislation that is "un-American" even if it must defy the people's momentary will.

For Coleridge the Idea of the Constitution is ultimately a universal arising from human nature. He believed that just as there is an essential proper nature, or constitution, of man, so there is a similar proper Constitution of the body-politic. The English Constitution is the particular manifestation in England of the universal Idea of the State. The Idea has a philosophical and ethical, as well as a psychological and historical dimension. But according to Coleridge's "method" there is little to be gained from discussing political universals in the abstract. They can be profitably studied only as they are reflected in the particular institutions of a living political organism. In the real world, universals find their expression in particulars. When proper method is followed, Reason enlightens the Understanding, but does not supplant it. Coleridge sought in *Church and State* to suggest the universal constitution by analyzing the concrete institutions of England in 1830. This analysis is a superb example of the method at work.

25. Ibid., p. 35.

CHAPTER 6

The Idea of the British Constitution

Coleridge saw the English Constitution as a durable balance of forces that reflected the Idea, or fundamental political principles, held by Englishmen over several centuries. This balance, the ruling principle of the Constitution, he called the *lex equilibrii*. Coleridge saw three social elements or tendencies that must be properly balanced against each other: "Permanence" and "Progression," "Church" and "State," and "Active Power" and "Potential Power."

The first balance, Permanence versus Progression, expressed in a theoretical formula Coleridge's opposition both to the French Revolution and its reactionary opponents. Unfortunately his formula seems to have been misunderstood, most notably by John Stuart Mill in *Representative Government*. By "Permanence" Coleridge meant all the tendencies within a society that seek to contain the various energies of national life within fixed, systematic channels. Such is the role of laws, institutions, and even customary practices, habits, responses, and feelings. "Progression," on the other hand, does not mean progress or improvement, as Mill seemed to believe, but rather refers to volatile elements in the society—elements not fully comprehended within the existing social, political, and legal structure. These are the elements that, in seeking a proper place for themselves, inevitably bring about change, if not progress. In any good society, Coleridge argued, there must be a constant interplay and a proper balance between these two impulses. Without the energetic forces of Progression there can be no vigor, no liberty, no improvement in material well-being. But while institutions must always yield to change they must not change so quickly that the society slips into economic, political, cultural, or moral anarchy. The tendency toward Permanence is the means by which the society captures and holds fast the achievements of the past—practical accomplishments that must not be lightly sacrificed to fitful experimentation.

Coleridge sought by historical example to illustrate the results of an imbalance of these two basic tendencies. Republican Florence, a splendid hotbed of genius and innovation, failed precisely because it was incapable of containing its wondrous talents within any abiding constitutional order. Venice, on the other hand, developed a structure so rigid that it ultimately smothered all vitality.

As Coleridge surveyed contemporary English society, he saw Permanence represented by the major landed magnates, Progression by the commercial classes. Permanence was tied preeminently to the land. The wealth of the mercantile, manufacturing, and professional classes, on the other hand, was "personal" and resided mainly in their skills and reputations. A man who wished to secure his wealth and position always turned to land and in so doing allied himself to those interests concerned primarily with maintaining wealth and position rather than acquiring it:

> To found a family, and to convert his wealth into land, are twin thoughts, births of the same moment, in the mind of the opulent merchant, when he thinks of reposing from his labors. From the class of *novi homines* he redeems himself by becoming the staple ring of the chain, by which the present will become connected with the past, and the test and evidence of permanency be afforded. To the same principle appertain primogeniture and hereditary titles, and the influence which these exert in accumulating large masses of property, and in counteracting the antagonist and dispersive forces, which the follies, the vices, and misfortunes of individuals can scarcely fail to supply. To this, likewise, tends the proverbial obduracy of prejudices characteristic of the humbler tillers of the soil, and their aversion even to benefits that are offered in the form of innovations.[1]

1. Coleridge, "Church and State," *Works*, 6, 39.

In the political institutions of England, the House of Lords represented the great landed permanent interests, Commons the commercial and progressive. The gentry, or minor barons, played an interesting role in Coleridge's analysis—a role similar in some ways to John Adams' Senate. The gentry were the balancing element between the two major antagonist forces and served to prevent a head-on collision. They were moderately wealthy landowners and were always represented by a sizable minority in Commons. Their presence in the lower house served to dampen the ardor of the more radical majority. Yet their parliamentary affiliation with the commercial interests strengthened these interests and indeed themselves against the greater landlords.

Between the antagonistic forces of Permanence and Progression, the King was the "beam of the scales." He united these opposing, but not contradictory forces in a common focus of loyalty.

If the antagonistic forces were to be kept in proper balance it was important that the balancing be facilitated by the machinery of political representation. Coleridge saw certain practices and conditions leading inevitably to an imbalance between Permanence and Progression in the legislature and a consequent deterioration of the body-politic. He named three specific situations he considered unwholesome:

1. The granting of political power to those without substantial property. The possession of property does not guarantee that a man is unusually intelligent, but it does imply that he has some measure of prudence, self-control, and probity. Without these qualities, intelligence becomes a menace. A property qualification assumes, Coleridge carefully added, that new talent will be allowed a fair chance to acquire property.

2. The continued exclusion from political power of any group that has come into property, this exclusion being based upon grounds that are irrelevant to ability to exercise political power prudently.

3. A gross disproportion between the parliamentary representation of the two antagonistic interests and their respective influence throughout the nation. Coleridge firmly believed that the legislature should represent interests rather than numbers.

The first caveat—political power must never be held by those without property—reflects Coleridge's fear of "mobocracy." Although he was clearly not against giving radical elements a place, he definitely opposed handing preponderant political power to those whose lack of possessions would give them, he feared, little stake in the country and make them particularly susceptible to the temptation to use their power to remedy their poverty or vent their resentments. Coleridge's sentiments seem reactionary today, but one should bear in mind the material and intellectual state of the lower classes in his day. It was not until 1884 that the bold step of nearly universal male suffrage was finally hazarded in England.

Coleridge proposed an additional restriction on suffrage less easily explained away by historical circumstances. He maintained that education should not be a substitute for property as a passport to political power. Intellectual achievement, in his eyes, is no guarantee of fitness to govern. Despite his great emphasis on education as a means for preserving the State, he was not willing to tie political power to intellectual attainments alone. If it were true, he argued, that intellectual ability is a sure indicator of practical wisdom and moral character, then the Chinese system of an educated bureaucracy chosen by open examination would be ideal. But for Coleridge intellectual prowess, political wisdom, and integrity are not necessarily conjoined. This point will be discussed more thoroughly in the next chapter, but it should be said here that Coleridge's distrust of the unpropertied intellectual in politics was not an ephemeral prejudice, but an important part of his whole view of politics. Of course it is also essential to his system that impecunious talent have the opportunity to acquire property and, once it has done so, achieve political power. Property qualifications protect Permanence from the reckless and the envious, while the circulation and enfranchisement of wealth give sufficient free play to the forces of Progression.

The third situation Coleridge deplored was, as we have seen, a gross disproportion between the parliamentary representation of the two antagonistic interests of Permanence and Progression and their respective influence throughout the nation. The legislature should, one way or another, represent fairly the various interests of the society. Democracy would distort the balance in favor of Progression. Yet it was not democracy that troubled

Coleridge in the parliaments of the early nineteenth century, but the stranglehold of the great landlords over both Lords and Commons. We have already mentioned Coleridge's views on the "stupid" Country Party. One might suppose he would have been eager for parliamentary reform. But he was not, and he justified his timidity by a rather sophisticated analysis of the relation between social and political power. Before hastening into simple-minded parliamentary reform, he argued, there should be careful consideration of all the new extra-parliamentary forces like newspapers and organized pressure groups that were beginning to have profound effects on parliamentary behavior. He contended that the influence of these new devices of popular politics would very likely more than counterbalance the apparent numerical superiority of the landed interest in Parliament. Although the representation of Permanence appeared superficially to be excessive, that would not be the difficulty in the long run. Coleridge was opposed to the Reform Bill as it was passed in 1832. He believed that the principle it contained would lead inevitably to universal suffrage and a permanent overrepresentation of Progression. Apparently, with so much change going on around him, he lacked confidence that Permanence would find other methods of maintaining its influence in Parliament.

Permanence versus Progression was the first of Coleridge's constitutional balances. The second was a proper relationship between the Civil State in a narrow political sense and what Coleridge called the "National Church."

The concept of a National Church has been regarded by some as Coleridge's most important and original contribution to political theory. His National Church is not actually a church in the usual sense of the word. It exists as an institution quite distinct from Christianity or any other religion. It is in effect a great national guild of the learned professions. Some such institution is necessary, Coleridge believed, in every well-ordered state regardless of whether or not it is Christian. In pre-Christian societies the pagan priesthood constituted the intellectual estate, or Church. If Coleridge were alive to observe modern Russia, he might regard the Communist Party as the National Church of the Soviet State. In England, he believed, such a Church had existed from the very beginning of the realm. It consisted of all the learned of all degrees, the "Clerisy" who together formed the educational establishment of the realm:

> The Clerisy of the nation, or national Church, in its primary acceptation and original intention, comprehended the learned of all denominations, the sages and professors of the law and jurisprudence, of medicine and physiology, of music, of military and civil architecture, of the physical sciences . . . in short, all the so-called liberal arts and sciences, the possession and application of which constitute the civilization of a country.[2]

This institution required an adequate portion of national wealth for its purposes. From earliest times, Coleridge argued, landed property in England had in effect been divided into two portions, the "Propriety" and the "Nationalty." The Propriety was that portion placed under the authority of the Civil State. It was leased out in entailed heritable portions to the aristocracy to be managed in perpetual trust for the benefit of the nation. The remaining portion, the Nationalty, was set aside for the maintainance of the National Church. Thus a certain portion of the nation's wealth was permanently set aside to support education and learning.

In modern times the commercially profitable professions such as law and architecture became self-supporting. But the Nationalty was still needed for the great centers of scholarship and instruction—the universities. And throughout the nation there remained a need for funds to support the local clergyman and schoolteacher. Coleridge believed these two figures existed ideally to perform essential and complementary functions in the local community. Both should be intellectuals by inclination and training. The clergyman, by virtue of rank and duty, was a gentleman whose functions brought him in contact with all levels of society. He and his family were meant to be a humanizing influence throughout local society, and by their example inspire respect for intellectual and moral cultivation. The schoolteacher, a younger version of the clergyman, was to instruct youth in the essentials of learning, patriotism, and morality.

2. Ibid., p. 53.

Whereas the role of the Civil State was to reconcile Permanence and Progression, law and freedom, the Church existed "to secure and improve that civilization, without which the nation could be neither permanent nor progressive."[3] The National Church was the necessary counterpoise, within the State in the largest sense, to the State in the narrow political sense.

It is only necessary to recall the *Lay Sermons* to realize how important Coleridge believed the function of the Church to be. With all the excitement that inevitably attended the magnificent progress of material civilization, it was little wonder that commercial values came to be so dominant. English culture could retain its balance, Coleridge believed, only if there was a corresponding vitality in the philosophical, religious, and artistic life of the nation. "Cultivation" could keep pace with civilization only if there were a vigorous National Church confidently secure in its values and spreading them throughout all levels of society.

Coleridge's admiration for the actual performance of the Church of England was at best tepid. But the Church's enfeeblement sprang, he believed, not from its own character, but from its relationship to the Civil State. A National Church can never perform its functions properly unless it is free from political meddling in general, and, in particular, unless its endowments are safe from the piratical incursion of hungry politicians. Before the Church of England could perform the functions of a National Church it would have to be protected from the political place-hunting that was so notable a feature of its operations. Hence the National Church should not be molested by the Civil State. Its trust is too awesome and its treasures too sacred to be subject to the political power of the moment: "No interest this of a single generation, but an entailed boon too sacred, too momentous, to be shaped and twisted, pared down or plumped up, by any assemblage of Lords, Knights, and Burgesses for the time being."[4] Ideally the Church should govern itself. In England, according to Coleridge, its proper governing bodies are its own Houses of Convocation. The titular head of the Church is the King, who is thus the trustee of the Nationalty. Any attempt by Parliament to

3. Ibid., p. 52.
4. Ibid. p. 91.

tamper with the independence or endowment of the parishes, universities, and schools is a violation of the true Idea of the Constitution and, if successful, will plant the seeds of a ravaging disease within the body-politic.

Although the politicians of Parliament have no rightful control over the National Clerisy, the nation as a whole has the right to expect that each member of that learned body shall have no allegiance to any power outside the nation nor acknowledge any head other than the head of the English realm, the King. Failure to meet this condition is the only absolute disqualification Coleridge would impose on membership in the Clerisy.

Coleridge's general theory about the National Church is bound up with his particular notions about the appropriate place of the Church of England in his own time. His arguments about the proper educational role of the Church of England are extremely complex. Today the whole subject is antiquarian. Whatever the history of the matter, education in present-day England can hardly be said to be under the direction of the established Church. But the historical entanglements should not be allowed to obscure the basic principle Coleridge sought to assert, namely that a proper State must have an educational system extending through all levels of the society. The system must be maintained by men who devote their lives to learning and teaching, and whose financial and intellectual independence is secure against the incursions of political power. The State may properly demand loyalty but not conformity.

Coleridge's insistence upon the autonomy of the National Church clearly implies a limit upon the supposed sovereignty of Parliament. His third balance, between "Active" and "Potential" Power, made his constitutional pluralism explicit. In his State, there is, strictly speaking, no sovereign power. There are a number of groups or interests within the State. When the body-politic is healthy, the powers of these groups will be in proper balance. Within the civil regime Permanence will balance Progression, and within the national State, the Church will balance the Civil State. This balance is the true Constitution, and behind the Constitution is the Idea. It is the Idea, as noted earlier, that provides the standard for determining the proper balance. But who is the keeper of the Idea? Who constitutes the supreme court of appeal?

Who, finally, is sovereign—the King, the King in Parliament, or the National Church? According to Coleridge, none of these is legitimately sovereign. The King, it is true, is the symbolic head of the State. But he is the supreme judge neither within the Civil State, where he is only the "beam of the scales," nor in the Church, of which he is only titular head. Parliament is, to be sure, sovereign within the bounds of the English political regime or State in its narrow sense. But the larger State is subject to the constitutional ideal, and for Parliament to claim the power to alter the fundamental rules and institutions of the whole society would be gross usurpation. These rules and institutions are not "to be voted up or down, off or on, by fluctuating majorities."[5] Nor can the Church properly claim sovereignty. Although the Church as guardian of education is in a sense also guardian of the Idea, the Church does not govern, but teaches. The Church is properly always a school, never a court.

It can be said therefore that sovereignty is nowhere institutionalized in Coleridge's State. The State is healthy when its distinct interests are correctly balanced. There is a standard for this balance—the constitutional Idea. But there is no absolute ruler to enforce it. What prevents the unhealthy domination of one element over the others? Who ultimately guards the Constitution?

To answer this question, Coleridge introduced his concept of "Potential Power." To be healthy the State must maintain a proper balance between its competing elements. But this balance is unlikely to persist unless there is a reservoir of potential political power, which, although latent, is a sufficient check upon the individual interests of the politically energetic. Potential Power cannot exist unless various groups within society enjoy a significant degree of autonomy. Coleridge argued paradoxically that only a society with considerable anarchical tendencies can be stable. For if Potential Power does not exist, any government can rearrange social institutions to suit every passing whim. Under such conditions a State can scarcely be said to have any Constitution at all. There are no abiding arrangements. He who captures the government captures all. The result is not stability, but a series of violent oscillations from the despotism of one group to

5. Ibid.

that of another. Potential Power is not only essential to stability, but itself constitutes liberty. Coleridge maintained that aristocracy is more solicitous of liberty than democracy, that England, long a home of seemingly archaic corporate and class privilege, allowed much greater actual individual liberty than any of the so-called democratic countries of ancient or modern times—a sentiment Tocqueville and Mill were to make commonplace. There is less liberty in a democracy, Coleridge argued, because "a democratic republic and an absolute monarchy agree in this; that, in both alike, the nation or people delegates its whole power."[6] There is no place to hide. Whoever is ascendant momentarily in the civil order is sovereign in the whole society. But the English nation had delegated to the Civil State of King in Parliament "power, not without measure and circumspection, whether in respect to the duration of the trust, or of the particular interests intrusted."[7] Coleridge believed that England, to its good fortune, had always embraced so wide a variety of social elements and treasured such untidy arrangements for government that the realities of English politics bore some kinship with his ideal.

In arguing for Potential Power as necessary to a healthy State, Coleridge was not advocating some sort of anarchy. For he firmly believed there could be no Potential Power or indeed liberty at all in a society where the enjoyment of liberty was not closely tied to the acknowledgment of duties. If the State was to remain healthy and able to avoid both anarchy and despotism, there had to be widespread devotion to the public interest. The reserve power was meant to be devoted to the defense of the Constitution, not to random subversion of lawful authority or selfish pursuit of private interest at the expense of the public.

Put in the framework of Coleridge's method: the good society preserves its particulars. They are not to be annihilated in the manic desire to achieve tidy, rationalized uniformity. But the particulars cannot be an immense heap of little things. They have to be informed by a more universal principle in the body-politic —by the Idea of the Constitution. The Idea both preserves the individual elements and relates them. The Idea has to be guarded

6. Ibid., p. 86.
7. Ibid.

by the society itself, by both the people and their leaders. The people are to be sufficiently possessed by the Idea to be aroused only over the right issues. And, most especially, the classes that provide most of the leadership for both Active and Potential Power have to be trained in perception of and devotion to the Idea. Because this perception is not automatic and intuitive, because it requires careful intellectual and moral training, a good State cannot exist without the proper education of the whole people, especially the higher classes. Such an education is quite impossible, however, in the absence of an independent National Church devoted to the pursuit of learning and the cultivation of the society.

This then is Coleridge's grand constitutional synthesis. Permanence and Progression mingle to insure a stable yet vigorous civilization guided by men who combine good sense and sound education with a heavy stake in the continuing success of the society. An independent National Church is devoted to the intellectual cultivation and moral unity of the society—a society in which there is room for the distinctive individualism of persons and classes.

It is easy enough to take Coleridge's ideal polity as nothing more than a conservative apology for traditional English aristocratic society. In the eighteenth century England had been presided over by a large and remarkably open governing class. An insistent radical impulse was tempered with strong respect for law and legal process. Individual and local liberties flourished as nowhere on the Continent, and yet the Revolutionary challenge had shown an abiding national patriotism that seemed to unite all classes. The Church, for all its faults, had done much to enrich the quality of English life. Above all it had prevented that separation, so fatal to France, between intellectual and gentleman. Coleridge devoted much of his mature life to formulating the principles that would justify this English tradition, provide for its improvement, and defend it both against Revolutionary Utopianism and the emerging culture of mass commercial society. From this point of view his most radical proposals seem only imaginative attempts to salvage and adapt a traditional order. Those who interpret him this way do not necessarily deny his considerable influence on later writers with quite different political predilections. Coleridgean ideas were at work not only in Disraeli's "Young England," but among guild socialists and Keynesians as well. But Coleridge himself is cast in the role of spokesman for a world that was already passing away rapidly. Even while he was still alive many of his specific political proposals must have had a certain antique flavor. As an old man Coleridge sat in Highgate, "a kind of *Magus*, girt in mystery and enigma . . . a sage escaped from the inanity of life's battle."[8] Meanwhile the world was swiftly changing. He was still alive when the Reform Bill was passed in 1832. When the young Darwin set forth on the *Beagle*, Coleridge had three more years to live. The Crystal Palace went up only seventeen years after his death. It should be said for him, however, that he never so lost his grip on reality as to propose a revived Gothic society in the age of railroads!

But to treat Coleridge's writings primarily as an historical period piece, even if considerable influence on later thinkers is conceded, is to rob him of much of his significance in the present world, and indeed in his own. His political philosophy transcends the limits of his own historical vision. *Church and State* is more than a sentimental, if imaginative, defense of a passing order. Neither Coleridge nor any other proper Romantic could believe that any ideal, any vision of the good society, was complete forever. In their vitalist universe, after all, change was the one constant. Belief in final solutions was a form of philosophical naïveté generally reserved for the Revolutionary Utopians. As writers like Coleridge never ceased to point out, it was the besetting sin of all revolutionaries. But surely, for the conservative, melancholy nostalgia is no less a vice. It is a self-indulgent misuse of the imagination, a mental faculty that has other more urgent political tasks to perform. Coleridge's entire philosophy committed him to the belief that no political formula is finally perfect, but rather that each age must devise its own ideals from past experience, present needs, and emergent ideas. The good society requires a perpetual exercise of creative political thought, of what might be called the political imagination. Coleridge is a conspicuous example of a creative political imagination at work on the needs of his

8. Thomas Carlyle, "Life of John Sterling," *Works*, ed. H. D. Traill (Centenary ed. 30 vols. London, Chapman and Hall, 1899–1923), *11*, 52–53.

age. He could scarcely have believed that his own political prescriptions made it unnecessary for the same creative faculty to be exercised by others in the future.

Unlike some other Romantics, Coleridge saw no superhuman force that guaranteed the inevitable success of this creative process either for the individual or for the nation. Imagination could fail in politics as in art. If the imagination always had to be exercised, because there could be no final ideals, and if there was no supernatural force that guaranteed the inevitable success of the process, then it would seem to follow that the most significant task of political philosophy is to discover the conditions most conducive to the successful operation, in every age and society, of the creative political imagination. The next chapter examines *Church and State* from this point of view.

CHAPTER 7

The Constitution and Political Imagination

Church and State is first of all an imaginative and perceptive survey of the shifting balance of political forces in Coleridge's England. It provides an interesting insight into English constitutional history. It reveals something of what English politics were in 1830 and a great deal more about what Coleridge wished they were. What results is a general picture of what Coleridge believed would be a good society for his own time and his own country.

But Coleridge was attempting more. He sought to illustrate from a particular example the universal principles that must govern all healthy States. True to his method he could not provide a final vision of the perfect society—complete for all time and applicable in all places. According to his most fundamental principles, practical ideals can never be dictated by pure universal Reason alone. Universals must always be adapted to shifting particulars. Furthermore ideas themselves are ceaselessly dynamic. Thus no man and no age can expect to capture the whole of truth. The healthy society is characterized by the ceaseless adaption and reformulation of its ideals.

There are certain social and political conditions, the *lex equilibrii*, that must be maintained if the process of adaptation and reformulation is to continue successfully. Needless to say, these persistent laws of politics must be honored in a manner appropriate to the particular time and place. But to some extent they can be isolated and referred to as characteristics of any healthy State. The attempt to discover the universal working through the particular is of course typical of Coleridge's method. What resulted in *Church and State* is a fascinating combination of philosophical generality and concrete analysis, not dissimilar in its method to Aristotle's *Politics*.

What can be said of Coleridge's *lex equilibrii* as conditions essential for the healthy growth of any State at any time? Why, to begin with, did these particular conditions seem so important to Coleridge?

Throughout his writing Coleridge was preoccupied with two fundamental problems: how to achieve a political system at once progressive but stable and diverse but coherent. Not all his ideas on how to achieve these aims are unusual. Many are familiar in modern Western political theory. Several modern writers on constitutional government, for example, have made use of the notion of a "reserve" power not actively committed to the political battles of the moment, but capable of being summoned to defend the basic constitutional structure—the rules of the game within which the active contenders are expected to confine their competition. The very distinction between active and potential implies a limitation upon the supposedly sovereign power of active government. The distinction, as noted above, seems to place Coleridge among the pluralists. He was an early exemplar of two important strains in the political thought of the nineteenth century, both of which might be called pluralist. There were those who came to revolt against the whole notion of an omniscient and omnipotent sovereign power that was somehow expected to supervise the affairs of the whole society. Others, following Tocqueville, Mill, and Coleridge himself, believed that modern society was smothering personal action and responsibility. They felt that the modern State was self-defeating, for its effects were increasingly inimical to the individual and moral intellectual development that was, after all, the State's ultimate purpose and justification.

It was the fear that modern society would overwhelm all individuality that explains at least part of Coleridge's solicitous attitude toward property. Diversity and individuality can be preserved, Coleridge argued, only in a society with substantial private wealth. It was not that he was unduly impressed by the virtues bestowed by wealth—particularly as distinct from breeding and cultivation. Indeed he despised the commercial ethic that saw wealth as the natural reward of virtue. He can scarcely be said to have been insensitive to the abuses of capital in his own day. But those who would eliminate property to cure its abuses are, again, "madmen . . . digging or blowing up the foundation of a house in order to employ the materials in repairing the walls."[1] Undermine property, Coleridge argued, and metapolitics bolstered by plebeian envy would soon produce an atomized society of standardized abstractions.

Without substantial wealth in the hands of individual families, there can be no effective Potential Power, for there would be no men sufficiently independent to offer sustained criticism and resistance to government policies. Dissent is not likely to flourish when economic ruin is added to the other penalties normally incurred by dissenters. The aristocracy can at least afford to be eccentric. And by their patronage they can offer refuge to others. Coleridge, for all his faults, was never anyone's hack. But as a young man he knew what it cost to be a radical and to lack financial independence. His own modest security was finally achieved only through the enlightened patronage of the Wedgewoods. He would not have fared as well with a parliamentary commission. He defended an order in which there would be many Wedgewoods, and at least occasionally a Coleridge.

Perhaps the security of private wealth is less necessary today than it used to be. It is doubtless fair to say that the universities and foundations are on the whole remarkably tolerant and seem to resist the temptation to impose standards other than intellectual discipline and honesty. Perhaps even the government nowadays is more tolerant of the unusual. But committees are always clumsy. Creativity needs privacy and silence. Moreover, every corporate body must inevitably have its basic orthodoxies. Few can escape entirely from the restless tyranny of fashion. The disturbing chronicle of the blacklisted Hollywood writers illustrates that some degree of economic independence is not altogether superfluous to the dissenter.

Pluralism generally implies much more, however, than the defense of private rights. When pluralism reached its apogee at the beginning of the twentieth century, it involved nothing less than

1. Coleridge, "Lay Sermon," *Works*, 6, 217. See Ch. 1, note 31.

a searching examination and attack on the whole juridical notion of sovereignty. The sovereignty of the people was declared an illusion, as was the expectation that any government acting in the people's name could supervise the affairs of modern society. Walter Lippmann, for example, doubted the competence of any government to oversee the multitude of national affairs, and especially doubted the ability or desire of the supposedly sovereign public to direct such a government.[2]

Coleridge anticipated many of these later views, but held countervailing views on the necessity for national ideals and leadership. Pluralist writers are sometimes justly accused of tacitly presuming a natural spontaneous harmony of interests and thus ignoring the chief difficulty of politics—the achievement of a consensus of loyalty and policy from among conflicting elements. They are said to believe that no national "plan" is necessary, and that particular groups can be expected to work out their limited problems by private bargaining. Coleridge, however, can hardly be said to have assumed that a good society could be achieved and maintained absentmindedly. While he believed that individual and corporate liberties are essential to the good life and the good society, he had no faith in the automatic benevolence of mindless, undirected social and economic processes. One need only recall his bitter criticisms of the workings of the free market. For Coleridge it was essential that against the rampaging "Spirit of Commerce" there be placed the self-conscious "Spirit of the State."

His Spirit of the State is not some shadowy Hegelian necessity. It is the reformulation, for a particular time and place, of realistic ideals of social and individual good. The great ideas that Coleridge believed had always governed human life—ideas of freedom, beauty, truth, and, more particularly, the Social Contract and the Constitution—must be adapted imaginatively to the demands of a particular moment. Coleridge found the moral of all history in Proverbs 29:18: "Where no vision is, the people perisheth."[3] Visionary ideals must both criticize and ennoble the present and point to the future. But if they are to exist and ful-

2. See especially the early writings of Walter Lippmann, for example, *The Phantom Public* (New York, Harcourt Brace, 1925).
3. Coleridge, "Church and State," *Works, 6,* 61.

fill their purpose, ideals have both to be imagined and effected by individual men. The successful exercise of political imagination cannot take place without men of vision who collectively fulfill the ancient conditions of power, wisdom, and virtue. The ceaseless adaption and reformulation of ideas can be accomplished only if there are leaders in the society trained philosophically to perceive ideas and employ them correctly. They must be trained, on the one hand, not to lose the universal in a heap of particulars and, on the other, not to war against individuality in the vain attempt to marry dead universals to living societies. Of course the State needs not only imaginative leadership, but a general population responsive to such leadership. The whole people must be inculcated with that moral self-respect and sense of civic duty without which decent government is impossible. Moral and religious education is thus, for Coleridge, the essential basis of the State. The National Church exists to provide this education, not to govern, but to train "for Publick employment both in Church and Civil State."[4]

Thus Coleridge's pluralism does not carry the implication that society needs no overall leadership and direction. For Coleridge as for Rousseau, there must be a general will. But it is to be formulated not by the assembled multitude, but by the political imaginations of educated men functioning within a balanced constitutional structure. Coleridge is a pluralist not because he denies the need for national leadership, but because he believes that some leadership and power must be kept outside the normal political channels of the Civil State. Otherwise the temptations of power may prove too great and the Constitution may be sacrificed to the greed or good intentions of those who momentarily wield active power.

But if there must be a general will, there must be some means of ultimately reaching and imposing policy. Hence questions of leadership and power are central in Coleridge's theory. In considering these questions Coleridge demonstrated his allegiance to property by insisting that suffrage should be tied to property. In

4. The Charter of the Collegiate School—later Yale University, October 1701. *Documentary History of Yale University*, ed. Franklin B. Dexter (New Haven, Yale University Press, 1916), p. 21.

all such matters, "Men . . . ought to be weighed not counted."[5] Coleridge advocated limited suffrage, not because he was reactionary, but because he was certain that government by the impecunious many would soon result in the destruction of constitutionalism and personal liberty. Constitutionalism, for him, meant the preservation of variety within the State, of diverse distinctive groups and classes leading their lives in harmonious interdependence but not dissolved into some universal undifferentiated Jacobin abstraction. Coleridge was not the last to fear that democracy would destroy individuality and constitutionalism.

Today the belief has become thoroughly implanted in the public consciousness that universal suffrage and government by consent are inextricably tied together. At least in advanced civilizations any system of government that does not call for frequent electoral contests and universal suffrage is automatically assumed to be ruling without the consent of its subjects. The motions of universal suffrage have become indispensable to mobilizing political consensus. Since Coleridge believed a State not only ought to be, but had to be based upon consensus, he would have had to accept universal suffrage in the present-day world.

Of course there were many in the last century, most notably Tocqueville, who foresaw this development. Tocqueville and those like him saw the inexorable necessity of democracy, but nevertheless feared its consequences. Today the old fear of majority tyranny is still present in one form or another. But democracy, property, and constitutional liberties have, after all, managed to coexist for a long time, at least in Britain and the United States. Democracy has not fulfilled the promise of Jacobin equality.

In retrospect the fears of Coleridge and others appear to have been greatly exaggerated. Why? Is it perhaps because universal suffrage has not in fact resulted in government by the people? This is a complex question the answers to which are subject to endless qualification. But there has been no dearth of writers all through the twentieth century who have pointed out that democratic forms do not automatically result in government by the

5. Coleridge, "Church and State," *Works*, 6, 212.

people. In a democratic country, to be sure, the electorate must be won over. But the means of influencing the electorate are increasingly denied to those who cannot command financial support. Money still seems to talk—perhaps more loudly in a democracy than elsewhere. Coleridge himself noted how profoundly the new power of the national press and the consequent possibility of mass and national pressure groups had undermined the dominance of the landowners in Parliament—all without a single change in the electorate. In short, Coleridge's first condition for preserving Permanence and Progression—power tied to property—can hardly be dismissed as obsolete. Is it, however, justified? Even if it is taken for granted that popular government is an illusion and that elites are inevitable, it does not follow that power should go to property rather than educated intelligence.[6] Coleridge's emphatic opposition to the granting of political power on the basis of intellectual attainment alone is the most surprising element in his whole system. He seems not only to be turning on his own kind, but denying his own emphasis on intellectual cultivation as indispensable to national health.

It was a fundamental belief with Coleridge that Reason unencumbered by property is dangerous. He was wary of intellectuals whose inventiveness is unfettered by tradition or concern for their own private losses. He feared their lack of experience in the practical world. He feared their impatience with stubborn individual facts. Above all he feared their penchant for tidy theories. These were the men who had brought on the Terror. These were the men who would uproot the most basic institutions of a society for the sake of an intellectual whim. Coleridge's fear of the intellectual in politics, I suspect, had much to do with his emphasis upon the National Church.

There were several reasons for a conservative writer in 1830 to distrust the property-less intellectual in politics. Modern political intellectuals, as such, made their debut in France during the eighteenth century. Their performance was not reassuring to conservatives. On the whole they were hostile to the established order, and in the long run their ceaseless criticism did much to

---

6. It is essential in Coleridge's system, of course, that there be "circulation," that new talent have access to wealth.

destroy the *ancien régime*. For a conservative constitutionalist what may well have been most alarming about the French intellectuals was not their criticism of abuses, but their underlying sense of hostile alienation from the whole social structure, an alienation that so easily converted clamor for reform into passion for revolution. And like many a modern Communist artist and intellectual, the *philosophe* persisted in deliberate and hostile rejection in spite of personal success and even adulation within the very system he sought to destroy.

Despite the flurry caused by such figures as Price, Paine, and Cartwright, or the enthusiastic preaching of the young Pantisocrats, the English intellectual in Coleridge's day never played a role comparable to that of his French counterpart. During the Revolution and the years immediately following, the established order in England was not confronted with criticism that was at once so widespread, so destructive, and so brilliant. Indeed it might be said that the best minds in England were generally devoted to the defense, rather than the destruction of the established order. One can think of any number of reasons why this should have been so. A chief cause was probably the relative role and condition of the Church in the two countries.

In order to examine the divergent roles of the Church in England and in France, it is necessary to go back to their common medieval heritage. In the traditional Christian society of the Middle Ages, the Church obviously performed a number of vital social functions. To begin with it provided for spiritual, charitable, and educational needs. It provided opportunities for impecunious talent, and above all, like the modern party, it was a home for the intellectual. It provided him with a comfortable haven where he was free, within the bounds of a generally acceptable orthodoxy, to pursue the life of the mind in safety and comfort. Furthermore the Church gave the intellectual not only a berth in the society, but great power as well. Hence the intellectual was very much a part of the established order, with many good reasons for wishing its preservation.

The Reformation brought the first great schism of the intellectuals. For one party or another the established Church became the abominable and despicable champion of error and persecution. Reconciliation was out of the question. The disaffected intellectual hence remained outside the established order and hostile to it. In France, Protestantism was suppressed, but the habit of hostility to the Catholic Church persisted, or at any rate was renewed by the partisans of nascent modern science. The "New Philosophy" provided a fashionable modern ideology for the disaffected. Under its banners Voltaire commenced the war of the intellectuals against the Church, which eventually expanded to include the whole established order of the *ancien régime*.

In England, as everyone knows, the development was different. The English settlement was not a clear doctrinal victory for anyone, but a loose compromise. After the fierce struggles of the seventeenth century the Church of England was purged of extremists and settled down into the vague "broad" middle. The clerical hierarchy became increasingly secularized and lost much of its centralized power and independence. The intricate network of places and livings became a major source of spoils and thus inextricably involved in the political life of the country. The English Church continued to reconcile the intellectual to society, if anything more efficiently than before the Reformation. The clergyman had long been a gentleman, but now he was tied to the established order not only by his rank, but by his family.

The British, chiefly it seems by regarding all criticism of Christianity and the Church as bad taste, managed to preserve the "broad Church" in its traditional integrating role throughout most of the eighteenth century. By the French Revolution, however, a new and hardier breed of antagonist had appeared, and in the years after Napoleon it became apparent that the great broad-Church compromise was in danger. Tom Paine might be dismissed as a national village atheist, but Bentham, James Mill, and their friends were more formidable. They saw the Church as the mainstay of a corrupt and absurd social and political order. They had neither respect nor sympathy for religious feeling. The integration of the intellectual into the Establishment was, to them, his corruption.

The intellectual comprehensiveness of the Church was disturbed by more than the appearance of distinguished and hostile secular intellectuals. Perhaps a more serious difficulty was posed by an embarrassing rebirth of Protestant religious fervor among the middle and lower classes. The militant resumption of evangelical enthusiasm, both within and outside the Church, made the task of comprehension vastly more difficult.[7] In short, both the revival and decline of religion served to swell the ranks of intellectuals and politicians hostile to establishment. In addition there were many within the Church itself who were outraged at its complacency in the face of internal corruption and its apparent indifference to the plight of the new industrial poor. The clamor for disestablishment grew all through Coleridge's lifetime. As he grew older he devoted more and more of his thought to justifying the special position of an established church. The idea of the National Church and its Clerisy represents the culmination of his thinking.

Coleridge sought to demonstrate that an established National Church is not a mere historical accident, but an integral part of any well-adjusted State. It is foolish, Coleridge believed, to ask why the State supports one sect over another. The Church of England is not just another sect. Indeed the National Church, according to its essential nature or Idea, is not a religious institution at all. It is a secular estate of the realm. If the Church of England is Christian, that is a fortunate historical accident. But if the English had continued to paint themselves blue and worship the sun, there would still need to be a Church of England:

> as the vine, with its prop may exist, though in less perfection, without the olive, or previously to its implantation;— even so is Christianity, and *a fortiori* any particular scheme of theology derived and supposed by its partisans to be deduced from Christianity, no essential part of the being of the national Church, however conducive or even indispensable it may be to its well-being. And even so a national Church might exist, and has existed, without, because before the institution of, the Christian Church;—as the Levitical Church in the Hebrew constitution, and the Druidical in the Keltic, would suffice to prove.[8]

According to Coleridge the Church of England is not a theological position. It is a national institution, essential to the State,

---

7. It is often asserted, on the other hand, that that same revival provided the antidote to Jacobinism among the lower and middle classes.

8. Coleridge, "Church and State," *Works*, 6, 60.

made up of all those concerned with the pursuit of knowledge. Through this doctrine Coleridge hoped to secure the Church from the inevitable shocks of sectarian theological controversy. He was perhaps the first in England to perceive the impending war between scientific criticism and "Bibliolatry"—a conflict that he knew would be foolish and unnecessary and that wearied his spirit. All the more reason, no doubt, for his desire to separate the Church from sectarian religion.

Coleridge desired to free the Church not only from sectarian, but from political entanglements as well. We have his opinion of the "place-hunting, discreet-correct dignitaries." But how could the clergy be otherwise, when livings were a mainstay of government patronage? The Church had to become autonomous. The community of the learned had to be freed from the financial and political meddling of Parliament.

Coleridge believed it was necessary not only to separate the purely political State from the Church, but also to separate the Church from the State. While his Clerisy should be free from government interference, they should be careful to resist the temptation to convert their immunities from the civil regime into power within it. This was, in Coleridge's opinion, the besetting sin of the Roman Church. Its constant tendency was to convert itself from a Church into a Civil State. As a result it either became itself the State or a subversive State within the State. These temptations have to be renounced of course if the autonomy of the Church is to be preserved. No civil government can tolerate a rival in its own sphere. Preservation of the proper constitutional balance depends upon mutual restraint on the part of both Church and State.

Coleridge had further reasons for keeping his National Church out of civil affairs. He came increasingly to believe that, for the sake of knowledge, the world of learning and the world of politics should refrain from too much intimacy. The study of philosophy, he believed, had suffered gravely from the increasing tendency of scholars to turn into journalists, unable to do without the applause of the vulgar public. Political philosophers were now expected to be political agitators. It was doubtful, Coleridge felt, that politics had been much improved by these incursions. Certainly philosophy had suffered much. The degraded state of contemporary philosophy was Coleridge's constant complaint. Philosophy offered no broad standard to expose the partial views that plagued contemporary politics. Again and again he returned to the cause of intellectual debility—the want of a truly philosophic class devoted to the dispassionate pursuit of truth.

Do Coleridge's ideas about the National Church have relevance in the contemporary world? Certainly his plans for the Church of England seem unrealistic in retrospect. Probably the chief stumbling block was religion itself. Christianity may be only a fortunate accident grafted onto the Idea of the Church, but the graft has taken. The Church can never be far separated from Christianity, and the attempt to be both comprehensive and religious seems to have failed. As long as the Church has any religious dimension, it is bound to be involved in divisive sectarian controversy, on the one hand, and to alienate the secular intellectuals, on the other. It would seem that the Church of England, however broad, can never become the general guild of the intellectuals in the contemporary world.

Why was Coleridge blind to this fatal weakness? No doubt he was sentimental about the Church. Furthermore he still hoped that the German Idealism which he sought to bring to England would eventually produce a new synthetic philosophy—a philosophy whose wholeness of vision would transcend the partial views of contemporary science and religion and restore coherence to the intellectual universe. Once again philosophy would rule and give a meaningful place to all branches of knowledge. Coleridge dreamed of effecting such a synthesis himself. A Church possessed by such a view could restore medieval unity and once again comprehend all those engaged in the labors of the mind.

If his hopes were extravagant, so were his fears. The Church of England was heir to the immense cultural wealth embodied in its own Christian past. Coleridge believed that if education were separated from the Church that wealth would be lost to the society. What, after all, could replace the Church of England—a Benthamite school system, mechanics' institutes, "lecture-bazaar" universities? Religion, Coleridge argued, has one great advantage as a means of education. By parable and symbol, backed by the authority of faith, its most complex truths can be adapted to all levels of intelligence. Hence faith makes every man a philosopher in conduct if not in intellect. Thanks to religion the behavior of the masses is informed by principles their intellects could never possess. Thus the character of a culture is always determined by its popular religious faith. "In fine, religion, true or false, is and ever has been the centre of gravity in a realm, to which all other things must and will accommodate themselves."[9] In the absence of Christianity few humane influences would reach the common man.

Both the hopes and the fears proved excessive. Despite some magnificent attempts Idealism did not succeed in restoring a medieval coherence to intellectual life. And the idea and function of the National Church persists even though the institution that once embodied it no longer appears to do so. In England and America no religious institution can today claim to be Coleridge's National Church. But what of the great private universities and schools and indeed the entire State educational structure? Private educational institutions possess an immense Nationalty, favored by numerous exemptions from taxation and control. Universities and foundations still give a home to the intellectual and serve to collect his loyalties within the established social order. The National Church has become secularized into the nonsectarian university and school. College presidents are the bishops of the modern world.

The transformation explains why, although Coleridge's title is *Church and State*, his book is more interesting today for its insight into the problem of academic freedom and the role of the academic in political life than for what it says about the separation of Church and State. The book's immediate inspiration, if we are to believe Coleridge, was his desire to illustrate why he opposed giving the Roman Catholic Church a free hand in England. There were, for Coleridge, some absolute limits to academic freedom, limits that he felt Rome did not honor. He believed that Rome was not a proper Church at all, but a bastard State. A member of the Clerisy could not be loyal to a foreign political State. Roman Catholics were unsuited to be members of the Clerisy. In spite of his fear of the Catholics, Coleridge's argu-

9. Ibid., p. 67.

ment leaned heavily toward academic autonomy. Without academic freedom, he believed, there could never be high standards of academic quality—a belief that seems well illustrated in countries where universities and governments have been intimately connected.

Coleridge was not heedless of the other side of the problem— the inability of any regime to tolerate the popular dissemination of ideas dangerously subversive to the established order. Indeed the man who stated that all the great revolutions in history were the result of the lucubrations of "recluse genius" was not likely to be unaware of the reckless power of ideas. Coleridge had treated the problem of free speech directly in *The Friend*. The scholar should be free to follow wherever his passion for truth leads. But he has no corresponding right to disseminate incendiary ideas in a manner calculated to inflame public opinion. This view is not exceptional. Coleridge was more interesting when he argued that the philosopher's preoccupation with influencing immediate affairs is dangerous not only to the State, but to the philosopher as well. The academic should, Coleridge seemed to believe, always resist the desire to be too practical, to apply his ideas too immediately. It was the lack of serenity and contemplative withdrawal that Coleridge saw as the curse of the intellectuals of his age. It led them again and again to those hasty and partial views that were so dangerous to the balance of society.

Ultimately, however, the only real defense against false ideas is true ideas. The successful pursuit of truth demands the cloistered walls of an autonomous National Church. This autonomy can never endure unless the Clerisy remembers its collective responsibilities to the nation, unless it realizes that the freedom to inquire and discuss requires the duty of intelligent self-restraint in popular dissemination. Coleridge saw such a sense of responsibility to the nation likely only if the intellectual is integrally tied to the society through institutions that guarantee his independence and promote his allegiance to the established order. He defended the Church of England because he believed that if it were disestablished the National Church itself would perish. If the established Church no longer fulfills the role of National Church the Idea itself is not necessarily obsolete. The Idea is expressed today in new institutions. The intellectual has found a new home in England and America. If his berth is unsatisfying, it is the conservative who should tremble. Coleridge was right, of course: nothing is more dangerous to an established order, more certain to change it, than a disgruntled Clerisy.

Coleridge's idea of the National Church suggests the whole fascinating question of the role of the intellectual in modern politics. It is his extraordinary suggestiveness that makes Coleridge, in politics as in many other fields, so rewarding a subject for close and imaginative study. *Church and State* is an excellent illustration. It is difficult to point to many investigations of the modern constitutional State that are at once so comprehensive in scope and so rich and provocative in detail.

Coleridge bore many resemblances to Rousseau. He wrote as Rousseau might have written after a long talk with the authors of the *Federalist Papers*. Coleridge's ideal State is based upon consent. Consent, however, is not enough. Consensus needs content. And as the State is continually confronted with change it needs imaginative leadership at its center—"energy"—to give it stability. The leadership should come not from the spontaneous intuition of the pure but simple populace, but from the trained intelligence of a large and open governing class—a class that combines property with cultivation and public spirit. Coleridge required further an autonomous National Church devoted to cultivating the society through education and the dispassionate pursuit of knowledge. And finally, in Coleridge's good society there must be elbowroom and variety. There must be many classes and many styles of life. The impulse toward social tidiness—the desire to level all classes into a homogeneous abstraction—was for Coleridge the fatal illness of modern political thought. A society devoted to such a program would inevitably impoverish itself. The world is forever changing. Ideals must always be formed anew. No single mind can grasp forever all of truth, no single ideal can compass all the good, no single style of living can embrace all the beauty and fullness of life. The good society, for Coleridge, contains many ways of life, yet with understanding and circulation among them.

It is the emphasis upon balanced diversity within the unity of the State that is the great heritage left by the conservative constitutionalists. It is this emphasis, I believe, that entitles them, more than democrats like Paine and Price, to be considered true prophets and apologists for modern Britain, and indeed, in a looser sense, for the United States as well. What is impressive about American society is not its democratic government "by the people." Fortunately America is not ruled by the people, albeit it is ruled with their consent. The splendid achievement of American society has been the generally peaceable incorporation, within a coherent unity, of a startling variety of groups and cultures. If we have achieved unity we have also preserved much individuality. This is the legacy not of democracy, but of constitutionalism —the tradition not of Paine, but of Burke.

Coleridge's way of looking at the world made him exceptionally suited to develop an adequate theory of the modern constitutional State. His method—the doctrine of Reason and the Understanding—reconciled him to continuous change. It made him tolerant of diversity, yet concerned with unity. His psychology allowed him profound insight into the nonrational forces that reinforce consensus. Finally his doctrine of the Imagination led him to be sensitive to the need for imagination and leadership in politics and the essential role of education in creating an adequate governing class.

In spite of the antique flavor of language and detail, there is much to be said today for Coleridge's conservative idealism. It is not altogether far-fetched to believe that the future freedom and health of American society depends not only upon the quality of its educational system as a whole, but especially upon its ability to educate a governing class in the Coleridgean sense—a public-spirited elite possessing talent, cultivation, power, a comfortable economic position. Tocqueville was probably right when he argued that grand designs in foreign policy can only be imagined and carried out successfully by aristocratic governments. Civilization has become so complex today that we seem to need grand designs in almost every area of the political community. Without a notable increase of political imagination in city and state government, for example, we can never hope to retain our traditional reliance on local initiative and local power. As the problems of "civilization" become more and more complex, the "cultivation" of educated leadership must become correspondingly intense. It should not be forgotten what Coleridge meant by education—not merely expertness, but the ability to see all things in relation to each other, to avoid partial views and one-sided values. The need for this kind of philosophic judgment is not limited to the international sphere, as contemporary city planning, for example, illustrates with depressing frequency.

A discussion of Coleridge's many excellences as a political theorist naturally leads to the question why they have been so little perceived. Of course not only Coleridge but most of the Idealists are neglected nowadays, except by those who attack them. Coleridge has had considerable effect on English political thought, although (John Stuart Mill notwithstanding) the debt has not often been acknowledged. There were numerous reasons why Coleridge was not taken seriously as a philosopher. His writing is wonderfully allusive, but often unclear in meaning and seldom professional in tone. For the sake of popularity Coleridge would have done better to have cultivated a more partial view. A balanced point of view, no matter how sane, seldom attracts attention. Historically there is no ideological slot for Coleridge. Nor is he useful for partisan purposes. He is too radical for conservatives and too conservative for radicals. His emphasis upon consensus and the "Spirit of the State" frightens not only the modern scholar preoccupied with totalitarianism, but the old-fashioned, liberal, "new conservative" as well. On the other hand, the "progressive," who favors a big State, is offended not only because Coleridge is skeptical about "act of Parliament reform," but because he is irremediably undemocratic. He appeals "for" the lower classes, but firmly believes that once one appeals "to" them the mob is at the door. With his lively sense of the limitations of human goodness, popular government for Coleridge can only mean "mobocracy."

His skepticism of democracy, however, does not render Coleridge obsolete for contemporary political theory. Indeed Coleridge merely anticipated the inexorable tendency toward elitism among the progressives themselves. Popular sovereignty was not the panacea anticipated by some, and faith in popular sovereignty has seemed to them more and more incompatible with the desire for positive and creative government.

Beatrice and Sidney Webb are excellent examples. They found it increasingly difficult to reconcile their faith in government by the people with their desire for government that would efficiently establish and maintain a society free from the evils of capitalism. More and more they came to have faith, not in the wisdom of the people, but in an elite of bureaucratic experts. The experts would be recruited democratically, presumably by the competitive examination of graduates from an excellent State educational system. The talented bureaucracy would, to be sure, rule for the benefit of the many. But the many would be asked for their consent only at stated intervals and on the broadest issues of policy. Meanwhile the government would continue its policy of gradually eliminating every vestige of inherited inequality, not only by creating opportunities for everyone, but by eliminating the possibilities for accumulating and transmitting substantial wealth.[10]

There is much in the Webbs that Coleridge would have found congenial. He would have agreed that society must be shaped according to an appropriate vision. He would not have objected to the energetic use of constitutional government to bring about that vision, although he would have been skeptical of government's ability to do so. Without any doubt he would have applauded the Webbs in their insistence that no solutions are final and that ideals must always be reformulated to suit new conditions. He certainly shared their oft-expressed concern that diversity be maintained for the sake of creativity within the society. But he would just as certainly have asked how it would be possible to retain diversity once its economic and social basis was destroyed. If society can never solve all of its problems, he might have asked, may there not some day be a need for another eccentric pair of Webbs with their privileged social position and their blessed one thousand pounds a year.

One suspects, finally, that Coleridge would not have got on very well with the Webbs. True, they favored an educated elite, but then so did Bentham. Coleridge had definite ideas about what constituted education as distinct from instruction. True knowledge is not merely information or skill. It is the ability to see the

10. A rather extreme statement of the Webbs' position can be found in Sidney and Beatrice Webb, *Soviet Communism: A New Civilization* (Reissue of the 2d ed. with the new introduction by Beatrice Webb, 2 vols. London, Longmans, 1941).

fullness of things in their proper relation. It results in the ability to avoid partial views and thus to achieve a balanced and sane judgment. For Coleridge, Bentham's elite would be a government of "talent" rather than "genius"—talent produced by hundreds of "lecture-bazaar" universities monotonously turning out their yapping, bumptious, and profoundly ignorant experts—experts as lacking in true learning and imagination as industrious in the pursuit of their dreary ideals.

Yet great as his aversion was to what he regarded as the shallow intellectuality of positivism, Coleridge offers little comfort to those who turn their backs on Reason. He might reject the dreary Left, but he would not be at home with the crazy Right. Fascism is, among other things, a cult of the irrational. It hopes to find in the violently active life of the hero the deeper truth that is lost to bureaucratic Utopia. But like most of the great Idealists, Coleridge would have none of this. Although a Romantic, he remained always a rationalist. He did not deny the fullness of emotional experience, but sought ultimately to include it in a larger order. He objected to absurd principles sanctified by feeling only. He detested "heroes."[11]

In the last analysis, Coleridge was the great apologist for aristocratic government—an aristocracy of humanists. Society, he believed, needs leadership—policy inspired by ideals that express the goodness of life in whatever dialect is appropriate for the moment. Education gives the governor the imagination to perceive a proper Idea of the State and the character to preserve it. Only a liberal education in its most humane sense fits man for government.[12] This ideal is never likely to be popular. It requires too

11. For further study of Coleridge's attitude toward heroes see my "Coleridge on Napoleon," *Yale French Studies*, 26 (New Haven, 1960–61), 83 ff.

12. Kathleen Coburn, who is surely more learned on the subject of Coleridge than anyone living, separates Coleridge's Toryism sharply from that of Wordsworth and Southey, "who came to identify themselves with the vested interests, and to be themselves laureates and patrons." Coleridge's conservatism was inspired by something beyond "opposition to reform and fear of the mob." He was a Tory because "his insistence on mental life as primary made him put educational before political rights and demands." Kathleen Coburn, "Poet into Public Servant," *Transactions of the Royal Society of Canada*, Section II, 3d series 14 (June 1960), 9. In

much intellectual discipline to be fascist, is too aristocratic for the democrat, too demanding for the privileged, and to the bureaucratic expert seems like pretentious dilettantism. It is not surprising that modern political theory has neglected Coleridge. Fortunately, however, practice is sometimes better than theory. Modern men are occasionally better than their principles.

Coleridge's system, it should be added, the two kinds of rights are in the final analysis essential to each other. The rest of Miss Coburn's article is an interesting account of Coleridge's service in Malta as "Segretario Pubblico del Commissionario Regio."

CHAPTER 8

The International Dimension

Nationalist theorists have always been confronted with the practical and logical difficulties which their devotion to the State raises for international relations. Most have eventually developed some theory of national coexistence. Until the Darwinists, nearly all nationalist writers proposed some theory or other based on the old observation, found in Plato, that a nation at peace with itself will be at peace with its neighbors. The "Father of Cultural Nationalism," Herder, seemed to believe that once national independence and political liberty were achieved for each nation all would live together in a naturally harmonious international order. Several decades later Mazzini professed much the same expectation, although he was more specific about the necessary preconditions. The optimism of both writers was buoyed up by their faith in inevitable progress. For Herder a divine energy, or *Kraft*, leads mankind through history to the elaboration in differing national cultures of *Humanität*— the copious potential of human nature. Later nationalist writers— Bernard Bosanquet for example—reflected the influence of socialism by adding the achievement of social justice within each nation to the preconditions necessary for peaceful national coexistence. Wilson's faith in national self-determination was simply another expression of the same optimistic view.

It is interesting that Coleridge never shared in the general current of nationalist optimism. He never saw the international world as Herder's placid garden where each nation dutifully flowers for the benefit of mankind. On the other hand, neither was his world the bloody Darwinian jungle of the imperialists.

It was closer to gardens as we know them, free neither from pests nor occasional murder. Indeed Coleridge's international garden is more Platonic than Romantic. The felicitous achievement of Nature requires unceasing contrivance by man. The successful political imagination is secondary rather than primary.

Coleridge dealt specifically with the problem of international relations in three chapters of *The Friend*.[1] He opened the subject by examining the theoretical implications of a famous international incident of the Napoleonic Wars. In 1807 the British navy attacked and destroyed the Danish fleet. The Danes were supposedly friendly neutrals, and the action was widely criticized at home and abroad as a flagrantly immoral violation of international law. The British government retorted that the existence of a large fleet about to fall into Napoleon's hands was an intolerable threat to British security. The action may have been immoral, but morality must be laid aside when the national interest is vitally affected.[2] Coleridge took up the theoretical aspects of the question and characteristically disagreed with both sides.

Coleridge asked whether there is any such thing as international morality, and, if so, what it demands. He began his answer with the rather misleading assertion that individual morality is not inapplicable simply because individuals act together. Moral principles apply to aggregates as well as to individuals. Although the law of nations is neither promulgated nor enforced, nations are under an obligation to behave morally in their relations with each other. But—and here Coleridge shifted his argument—the moral responsibilities of States are quite different from those of individuals. England's action against Denmark was not immoral,

1. Coleridge, "The Friend," *Works*, 2, First Section, Essays 10, 13, and 14.

2. The government's case was presented in the House of Lords on Monday, February 8, 1808, by Marquess Wellesley. See *Cobbett's Parliamentary Debates, First Series, 10* (London, Bagshaw, 1808), 342 ff. Wellesley's argument is actually based upon the natural law of self-preservation and is not incompatible with Coleridge's. The Wellesley referred to here was Richard Colley Wellesley, the eldest brother of the Duke of Wellington and an important political figure in his own right. He served both as Governor-General of India (1797–1805) and Foreign Secretary (1809–1812). This speech was his first in the House of Lords and is said to have been extremely effective.

for it is the highest moral duty of a State to preserve itself. He justified his position by returning to the old Platonic assertion that a good man is likely to be developed only in a good society. Indeed Coleridge seriously questioned, as we know, the reality of the concept of man abstracted from his national environment. Man separated from the particulars that give content to his humanity is for Coleridge such an abstract concept that it refers to nothing recognizable in human experience:

> In two points of view, I reverence man; first, as a citizen, a part of, or in order to, a nation; and secondly, as a Christian. If men are neither the one nor the other, but a mere aggregation of individual bipeds, who acknowledge no national unity, nor believe with me in Christ, I have no more personal sympathy with them than with the dust beneath my feet.[3]

Along with most nationalists of the nineteenth and twentieth centuries, Coleridge believed that a good society producing good men and a noble civilization cannot long flourish under an alien government that denies the people the rights, duties, and fraternity of citizenship. Remember the example of the Greeks. While free and independent they were "the benefactors of all mankind." When they lost their independence, even as prosperous and pampered subjects of the admiring Romans, their genius fled. "Alas! no Sophocles appeared, no Phidias was born; individual genius fled with national independence."

From this belief an inevitable conclusion followed:

> If then in order to be men we must be patriots, and patriotism can not exist without national independence, we need no new or particular code of morals to justify us in placing and preserving our country in that relative situation which is most favorable to its independence.[4]

Hence, Coleridge argued, the State is bound to observe no treaty that would destroy the State itself. Nor can the State be morally constrained from using force to prevent or remove a threat to its independence, not because international politics is

3. Coleridge, "Table Talk," Works, 6, 395.
4. Coleridge, "The Friend," Works, 2, 269.

amoral, but because it is in fact the highest moral duty of States to preserve themselves. A State is not simply another token on an international gaming board. The State encompasses an entire society and its culture. Its preservation is the highest duty of all governments and their citizens.

"But," Coleridge added, "the true patriot is aware that this object is not to be accomplished by a system of general conquest."[5] Preserving the State requires prudence—the wise Understanding. History teaches that the extension of the State to foreign interests and influences often marks the beginning of national enfeeblement. The preservation of a State is generally easier if it is surrounded by neighbors warm with respect and remembrances of past kindness. Even the destruction of a dangerous enemy is often soon regretted as it lessens the opportunities for diplomatic maneuver. Not infrequently those who are now enemies become allies.

But these are considerations of expediency. The morality of the situation is clear. It is the highest duty of the State to preserve its way of life, since only within this native context can the individual develop his human potential.

Coleridge's argument in *The Friend* has always seemed to me to be rather haphazard. He avoided the significant problem: that of the good man who is a citizen of a bad State, especially when that bad State is engaged in an unjust war with a good State. Nevertheless Coleridge's essential attitude is clear enough and thoroughly consistent with the whole of his political theory. His view of the State and hence of international relations was dominated by two of his most fundamental principles, one philosophical and the other psychological.

Coleridge was opposed on philosophical grounds to the kind of cosmopolitanism that seeks some form of universal State based upon principles applicable to all men in general. This kind of ideal seemed to him only another offshoot of the fatal science of metapolitics. Those who believe in a universal State governed by universal law are committing the old mistake. They are seeking to apply the abstractions of pure Reason without taking into account the innumerable and shifting particulars encompassed within any human community or single human being. The fatal

5. Ibid.

passion for the tidy abstractions of pure Reason leads men to ignore the reality of life and to pursue a bloody crusade against all particulars, against all national and personal individuality.

On the other hand, Coleridge was not content, as we have seen, to leave politics divorced from Reason. The State has its ideal, the Constitutional Idea, perceived by Reason. The national Idea does contain some universal elements. The *lex equilibrii* applies to all healthy States. But the universal principles are empty and barren abstractions until filled with the particular color and richness of an individual national culture.

Coleridge's deliberations, in this respect as in so many others, bring him remarkably close to Rousseau. Rousseau's *Social Contract* was written to express a universal ideal whose basic truths were applicable equally to all States. Yet Rousseau's ideal State was extremely small and self-contained. And even in the *Social Contract* Rousseau made provision for the cultural peculiarities of each State. In such later studies as *The Government of Poland* he adapted his ideal to the unique cultural character of a particular national State.

Of course Rousseau was not typical of many thinkers of his time. The rationalism of the French Enlightenment certainly had a strong cosmopolitan flavor. A system based on universals naturally tends to be unhistorical, impatient of peculiar nonrational traditions and institutions, and hence favorable to a universal State. On the other hand, this is not a necessary quality of a political Utopia based upon universal ideals. Plato and Aristotle, as well as Rousseau, believed that the ideal of a perfect State is universal, but they did not feel that this obliged them to urge a universal cosmopolitan State. In fact each believed that the achievement of the universal political ideal can only take place within a small, particular, and exclusive State. Though all were "Idealists," all had a strong sense of the limitations of human efforts to achieve the ideal. All believed that man can come closest to the ideal only within a finite State that absorbs his ultimate loyalties. Though Socrates had to die for truth, he could not in good conscience betray his State—nor could he imagine life cut off from it.

Neither Plato nor Rousseau, however, was a Christian. Neither was committed to the Augustinian concept of moral excellence achieved apart from politics or the State. The pagan philosopher offered salvation through political activity in the unselfish service of the State. The State in this sense was both State and Church. For the Christian this is blasphemous and incomprehensible. Politics is irrelevant, or at least incidental, to Christian salvation. The State is merely a convenience. Morality is at once personal and cosmopolitan. Men are not saved en masse; salvation is a personal affair for each man. All men, or at least all Christians, are equally loved by God; nationality is irrelevant to moral standards or obligations. The State may, for the sake of convenience, be national; but the Church, and hence morality, is universal.[6]

These two ideals, the pagan and the Christian, have existed side by side for centuries, and there have been a number of notable attempts to reconcile them. But it is questionable whether, aside from Coleridge, there have been many writers who have been so strongly committed to both positions at the same time. Coleridge devoted much of his energy to the preservation and rejuvenation of Christianity. He did his best to make his Idealism compatible with a reasonably orthodox Christian theology.

Coleridge's faith was so strong and so flexible that he saw no ultimate conflict between Christianity and philosophy. Such conflicts as had occurred, Coleridge believed, had been the result of the "plebification" of learning. Both philosophy and religion had been degraded by those busy nonentities who possessed a talent for the vulgar generalizations useful to journalism, but lacked the genius essential for profound philosophical thought. Give learning back to the learned, Coleridge argued, and religion will take care of itself.

It was to preserve both true philosophy and true religion that Coleridge urged an autonomous National Church. The autonomy of this learned guild would, he hoped, preserve the excellence of its thought. But this Church was given a special function within his State. He asked it to teach "civility"—the qualities that make the citizen loyal and dependable. Religion is indispensable to Coleridge's State. But what if this religion is dedicated to ideals that transcend and possibly conflict with the national Idea?

6. This extreme Christian ideal, as expressed by Augustine, has obviously been much compromised throughout history.

What if Christianity refuses to allow the mixed Idea of the State to cloud its pure vision of God? What, in short, if Christianity refuses to become a State Church?

Coleridge's position on the relation of Christianity to the State was as follows: the Christian faith or "Church of Christ" is an *ecclesia*, the communion of such as are called out of the world. The Church of England, which is only improperly called a Church at all, is an *enclesia*, "an order of men chosen in and of the realm, and constituting an estate of that realm."[7] Though Christianity has immeasurably enriched the English Church, it is not, theoretically speaking, essential to its existence. The olive tree enriches the nearby vine, yet they are not the same plants and can exist separately.[8] To have political effect, religious morality must become embodied in the Idea and consequent culture of the State. Otherwise religion is a personal matter irrelevant to politics and, one might say, to morality itself.

But Coleridge was not Paine or Voltaire. His religious sense was highly developed. Why then was he so eager to separate religion from education and from the State itself—a merely theoretical separation, which he admitted had never occurred in England and which he would have vehemently opposed if it had? Coleridge attempted to solve the tension between Christian ideals and the State with the same arguments he used in limiting the applicability of philosophy to politics. The highest ideals of religion, like those of philosophy, are too pure to be applied to the practical world of politics. Earthly life is too complex to be regulated by pure Reason alone. The State is not a Church. Religion joins philosophy—both banished to heaven. The philosopher gazes upward at them with love, but only confusion and woe will result from attempting to establish their reign upon earth.

Coleridge's nationalism may well have cost him much intellectual peace of mind. It is likely that he was not completely at ease with the role he assigned religion. So much of his philosophy is clearly universalist.[9] Unlike the nationalist Herder, Coleridge

7. Coleridge, "Church and State," *Works*, 6, 53.
8. See p. 114 above.
9. In a sense the whole question of the role of the Church of Christ in the State parallels the relation of pure Reason to the Understanding. In both cases, when it comes to the practical affairs of the world those ideals

was in no sense a relativist. This can perhaps be seen most clearly in the differences between the literary criticism of the two men. Coleridge did not find his critical standards in the unique genius of each culture.[10] On the contrary, he is hailed as the founder of a modern school of criticism which is primarily interested not in cultural peculiarity, but in universal canons of taste.

This universalism shows in his politics as well. While his sense of the limitations of earthly endeavor prompted him to fix upon the individual State as the only proper context for political life and standard for political morality, once he fixed his loyalty to the particular State it is interesting to note that the universalist elements inherent in his whole philosophy began to assert themselves. Unlike Herder, he did have a standard that applied in the last analysis to all States. No State can be exactly like another. But Coleridge certainly believed that some States are good and others bad. Herder argued that nations should be understood, rather than judged. Coleridge had no such notion. It bears repeating that Coleridge was not a cultural relativist. When he discussed the English State, it was presumably to illustrate an ideal Constitution as applicable to Venice and Florence as to Britain. And after a time it became somewhat unclear whether England was the illustration or the ideal—the universal particular.

Like Coleridge, Herder of course believed in loyalty first to one's own culture. But Herder also possessed a truly cosmopolitan appreciation for the genius of other nations.[11] There is a not-

and institutions that are universal in scope and perceived intuitively and personally by each man are properly made subject to those ideals and institutions whose scope is less than universal and whose determination demands intellectual discipline and practical experience. In the world of politics Coleridge was not a fideist.

10. Coleridge very definitely believed that there are transcendental standards for judging the excellence of poetry. See G. A. Wells, "Herder's and Coleridge's Evaluation of the Historical Approach," *Modern Language Review*, 48 (1953), 167–75, and, by the same author, "Man and Nature: An Elucidation of Coleridge's Rejection of Herder's Thought," *Journal of English and Germanic Philology*, 51 (1952), 314–25.

11. Herder did have his peevish moments. He was especially unimpressed by the Japanese, whom he described thus (salvaging his relativism only in a final phrase): "The Japanese, a people of Chinese tuition, but probably of Mongol origin, are almost universally ill-made, with thick

able lack of this second quality in Coleridge, which will become apparent as we turn to Coleridge's specific ideas on the coexistence of States.

To begin with, as we noted above Coleridge had no conception, sentimental or otherwise, of the value of man simply as man and nothing else. In addition, Coleridge was not indiscriminately fond of the citizens of nations other than his own. In fact his writings are filled with rather ill-natured remarks demeaning other nationalities. He respected the genius of the Germans from whom he had borrowed much, but regarded them as unsteady and given to excess. For the French he generally showed a most uncordial dislike. They had caused endless trouble for the world, and had little philosophical genius. They were bumptious masters of the superficial. He loathed the Roman Catholic Church and constantly spat at it with a venom just slightly less noxious than that reserved for "the APE" (Napoleon).

But this unneighborly crotchetiness had one advantage. For Coleridge, unlike Herder, did not blandly assume that nations, however different, would exist in unforced harmony. Coleridge had no faith in untended gardens! Not with so many weeds about! Thus he did not sidestep the problem of coexistence, but took it up in what for him was a direct manner.

Coleridge's conception of national coexistence was certainly more pessimistic than Herder's. It is interesting to speculate on the differences that were responsible for their contrasting views on this subject. Perhaps the most obvious difference is that whereas Herder was concerned with culture Coleridge dealt with politics. Coleridge united Herder's nation with a political State. When dealing with a subject as vast as the cultural history of all mankind, it is no doubt easy to overlook a number of disagreeable details. But war occupies such a prominent place in the history of States that it is difficult to avoid the conclusion that it is inevitable.

In addition there were fundamental differences in the philos-

---

heads, small eyes, stump noses, flat cheeks, scarcely any beard, and generally bandy-legged. Their form of government and philosophy abound with violent restrictions, suited only to their country." J. G. von Herder, *Sämmtliche Werke*, ed. Bernhard Suphan (33 vols. Berlin, 1887–1913), *13*, 218.

ophies of the two men. Coleridge's view of coexistence was not softened by belief in a Providential fate that justifies all history. History for Coleridge manifests evil as well as good, failure as well as success.[12] Herder believed that all national cultures realize a different version of *Humanität,* and that no one can judge among these contrasting expressions. Coleridge did not so limit himself. He postulated universal ideals even if they could be realized only within a limited context. Some nations, like England, were closer to the ideal than other nations which, like France, were far away indeed. In short, some nations are good and others bad. Herder used Providence to abolish sin; Coleridge acknowledged no such palliative for the harshness of history.

Herder and Coleridge shared one crucial attitude—both were strongly opposed to cosmopolitan ideals universally applied. But they justified this attitude by quite different arguments. As a relativist, Herder tended to believe that such ideals do not exist. His nationalism rested upon his observation that cultural vitality occurs only within a limited, particular context. Coleridge's position was more complex. He did not deny universals, but argued that they have practical meaning only within a context created by unique particulars. In this question as in so many others, Coleridge demonstrates his assertion that the distinction between Reason and the Understanding is crucial to his whole philosophy. When his ideal leaves heaven for earth, it becomes so mixed with the particulars of one people that it loses its universality and becomes a unique national Idea.

Regardless of these philosophical differences Coleridge accepted the fundamental postulate of nationalism: there are definite limits to the extent of political consensus. Coleridge believed that a worthy political society free and tolerant of diversity, and offering to the individual the ennobling responsibilities of citizenship, cannot exist except within a community of strong common loyalties. When a State is extended too far, he believed, coercion must tend to replace consent. Hence, while national States may be balanced and free, empires will be despotisms.

These nationalist ideas applied to international politics call for a world of separate States, each displaying a distinct national culture. Each State is charged with the moral obligation to pre-

12. See Chapter 3, n. 14.

serve itself. One of two conditions is characteristic of such a world. Either there is some fundamental harmony in man's nature or environment that results in world peace or whatever harmony does exist is insufficient to prevent at least occasional conflict. Nationalists like Herder and Mazzini believed in a fundamental harmony; Coleridge did not. He did not expect that Providence would ever abolish the tensions and imperfections characteristic of human life since the beginning of time. It was not so much that he believed war to be inevitable as that he believed it could only be avoided by the sincere vigilance of men of good will who possessed an imaginative grasp of reality.

The student of international politics is not likely to quarrel with Coleridge's expectations about a world of separate nation-states. The evidence of modern history is rather unequivocal about the nature of national coexistence. If the history of the past has any lesson for the future, it is that there will continue to be conflict among national States at least until there is a radical increase in the world's abundance and a drastic sweetening of human temper.

This cheerless prognostication raises the fundamental question: why should anyone defend or even tolerate concepts of the nation and the State that lead to such gloomy international consequences? In short, has nationalism not had its day and with it the theories of the State put forth by such writers as Samuel Taylor Coleridge?

CHAPTER 9

The National State Today

Coleridge's was a remarkably creative conservatism. It pointed at least as much toward the future as the past. For all his misgivings, he watched the passing of the traditional order with feelings not entirely devoid of enthusiasm. While he was certain that French attempts to create a new political framework during the Revolution were doomed to failure in practice because they were wrongheaded in theory, he never ceased to hope for a successful political reformation in England. Consequently he sought in his political philosophy not merely to applaud the wisdom of his ancestors, but to adapt it to the needs of a revolutionary world. A lifetime of study and speculation made him not only a defender of certain traditional arrangements, but a prophet of the kind of constitutional national State that was to develop in the nineteenth century. His vision was, for its day, a notable, if unappreciated, triumph of the political imagination. Does Coleridge's theory of the national State have any relevance to the political problems of today?

It must immediately be said that there is much in Coleridge that is almost totally irrelevant. Obviously his views on such matters as the relationship of major barons to minor barons, the educational role of the Church of England, or the special status of landed property have little immediate application. They are the particulars of his theory, valid for a single culture at a definite moment in its history. But Coleridge knew that particular institutions would always have to be recast into forms that reflected the enduring laws of politics in a fashion suitable to contemporary needs and styles. That was why he made leadership and imagination such vital elements in his political theory. I have argued in Chapter 7 that when the particulars are taken from his political theory there remains a consistent way of looking at the nature of a national State and a description of those elements and balances necessary to keep it in good health. Coleridge's general principles will in fact always be relevant in viewing a national State. The great question is whether the nation-state itself is still a creative political formula in our present-day world. Is nationalism outmoded?

The answer depends partly, of course, on how nationalism is defined. If nationalism is a doctrine which asserts that, in its external relations, every national State has the moral right to do exactly as it pleases, without regard to the consequences to anyone else or that, internally, the citizen owes unquestioning obedience to an authoritarian centralized government, regardless of the decisions that government takes, then it is relatively easy to show that nationalism is a retrograde political theory. On the other hand, if the definition of nationalist is to include all those who believe that political consensus can be achieved most successfully within a limited "national" community, then it must be allowed that nationalism has been one of the great creative forces of modern politics. In general the nation has proved so far to be the only context within which the elements of modern society can be organized in such a way that a reasonable degree of individual and group liberties is preserved. It is only within national contexts that the delicate balances essential to modern constitutional democracy have been achieved and maintained. The national State, as it developed in Britain and the United States and today exists in most of Western Europe, is surely the most successful attempt in history to achieve peaceful political consensus within societies that are at once so diverse and so politically conscious.

Nationalism can, after all, be distinguished from its perversions. Xenophobia is not an inevitable attribute of the nationalist. Patriotism is not necessarily warlike. Internal national solidarity does not mean external aggressiveness. Closely knit families do not all necessarily behave toward each other like Montagues to Capulets. Nor is it true that all who believe in constitutional democracy are enthusiastic for world government. Indeed, over the past century and a half it has generally been quite the contrary. The Battle of Britain was not won by advocates of world government. Churchill was more legitimately a nationalist than Hitler.

Nevertheless it is quite possible to acknowledge the historical achievements of nationalism and still regard it as a reactionary force that stands today in the way of further progress. It can be argued that we, like Coleridge, live in a world where the traditional political formula no longer provides an acceptably stable political system. Events in the twentieth century may finally have passed by Coleridge's national State, however admirably nationalist constitutionalism may have solved the domestic problems of industrial society in the last century. Today it is often said that nationalism has led to a situation that seems to threaten civilization and even life itself. On one hand the international system that has resulted from nationalism has been so unstable in the past that it seemingly makes war all but inevitable. Coleridge found war deplorable, but expected that wars would continue to occur in a nationalistic world. Since Coleridge believed consensus was only possible within the limited context of the national State, he was willing to accept the resulting international instability as the necessary price of domestic freedom. Today we cannot afford to be so complacent. Nuclear weapons have increased the possible costs of war to such a magnitude that peace has become an overriding concern. National independence, whatever its comforts, seems rather small-minded. To many, progress toward secure peace depends upon undermining national sovereignty and replacing its functions by international organizations pointing eventually to world government.

But even to those who are skeptical about world government, nationalism sometimes seems outmoded because a single nation-state can no longer, it seems, ensure either the safety or prosperity of its citizens. For military and economic reasons modern technology requires a context larger than the traditional State. While world government may be impossible, new, larger political units are essential. Both arguments, though fundamentally different, can be employed by the same people. Jean Monnet, for example, advocates European federation, but only as a giant step toward ultimate world government.

Anyone who would banish nationalism does, however, have to contend not only with a theory but also with a political fact. Like death, nationalism cannot be got rid of merely because it has unpleasant side effects. Indeed, it can be argued that nationalism is far more of a fact today than it was in Coleridge's world. To do away with national States, some form of vast supranational if not world government would have to be established. World government may be a daring program, but it is not a new idea. Today, it can be argued, it is less likely than ever to be realized. Had Napoleon succeeded in forging Europe into a superstate, it is conceivable that before the century was out the world might have been united under a single government, such was the relative power of Europe and the political passivity of most of the rest of the globe. Today political consciousness has spread to the masses of Asia and Africa, Western colonialism has retreated, and, for the moment at least, the imperialism of the Russians has been contained. Neither superpower is likely to establish world hegemony. The United States has always lacked the will to be master; Russia, with the United States against it, has lacked the power. In fact, both seem at the moment to be losing control of their own blocs. The world is probably farther from any form of cosmopolitan government than at any time in modern history. Certainly that is true of Asia, Africa, or South America. Local States may amalgamate into larger units, but external control will not be reestablished. Indeed, nearly all contemporary experiments in federalist regional groupings seem to have failed. In almost all parts of the globe, the national State is today the most relevant formula for political organization.

If the national State has declined anywhere, it is only in its old home, the Western world, and especially in Western Europe. Until recently at least, few politicians on the Continent have cared to speak openly against European union. Even the Gaullists, jealous as they are of French identity, have nevertheless ardently proposed their own blueprint for European political cooperation.[1] At times the struggle seems almost to be between the partisans of Europe and the enthusiasts for an even more grandiose form

1. This assertion seems somewhat undermined by Michel Debré, *Au Service de la Nation* (Paris, Stock, 1963). See for example Ch. 1, "Une Jeunesse Nombreuse."

of Atlantic union. Both economics and politics have nourished the general enthusiasm for a supranational community for Europe. The Common Market has convinced many of the advantages of a larger economy. The immense cost and complexity of military defense is another strong incentive to a breaking down of national barriers and the formation of a new international system no longer based on the sovereignty of the single nation-state. To many, in short, the old order seems clearly obsolete. There is, however, no agreement on the form the new order should take. It was at the beginning of the last century, during a similar period of uncertainty, that the modern concept of constitutional nationalist State arose as an alternative to Napoleon's ideal of a cosmopolitan bureaucratic State. Does nationalist theory, and Coleridge in particular, have anything to contribute to the current search for the proper forms for political community, or can the principles for new communities be found only after resolutely turning our backs on nationalism?

It is generally agreed that the most successful new form of political community beyond the nation has been achieved in the "supranationalist" European institutions, especially the Common Market. Here, it is often argued, is the modern institution from which the principles of a new international order must be derived. If they fail, it will be on account of the stupid blindness of recalcitrant nationalists and not because of any inherent weakness of the federalist idea. The guiding principles of these new communities seem uncompromisingly antinational. Indeed there is a strong tendency among the partisans of the new Europe to reject nationalist theory out of hand. What is needed for Europe, they argue, is not merely a new and larger nation-state, but rather an entirely new form of political community. To create a new European nation would only perpetuate a reactionary idea and an obsolete form; national States today are not sovereign, but "interdependent."

An appropriately modern European political community, the argument runs, should not be national, but "supranational." The Common Market (or European Economic Community) gives an indication of how a supranational institution works. It is not "sovereign." Its scope, though important, is limited, and for the enforcement of decisions it relies ultimately on the enlightened self-interest of national governments. Nevertheless it is more than a loose alliance. Eventually many decisions are to be taken by a form of majority vote. And most important of all there is the Commission, a permanent committee of cosmopolitan bureaucratic experts who not only administer, but have a most important role in initiating and drafting policy.

In comparison with national governments, the Common Market is strikingly free from popular control or participation. While there is a European Parliament, its effective power is limited, and in any event it is chosen not directly, but by the parliaments of the member States. In short, the EEC is governed by a bureaucracy of highly skilled international servants operating with great freedom within the framework of broad policies and procedures acceptable to the member governments. The Community is a government by technocrats rather than politicians, intelligence rather than popularity. Its officials are free from many pressures and considerations that harass national governments.

These arrangements have been remarkably successful thus far in harmonizing and integrating a European economy. Could such institutions actually succeed in providing the necessary direction for a European community without acquiring the rest of the paraphernalia of a national State? Is it feasible to place the decisive political power of a community in a government without making that government also the repository of national loyalty and legitimacy? Not according to the classic nationalist prescription. The larger the economy, the more likely it is that diverse interests will clash, the greater is the necessity for "energy" at the center actively promoting the reconciliation of interests, and the more necessary it is that that which purports to act in the name of the common good is endowed with popular support and the aura of legitimacy. National States are the only forms that have succeeded in creating sufficient consensus to legitimize power. Thus it would seem to follow that if Europe would unite its economy it must become a State: and if there is to be a European State, there must also be a European nation.

These prescriptions depend upon the assumption that consensus is so difficult to obtain naturally that it can never be achieved without that awesome web of institutions and loyalties that is the political infrastructure of the national State. Nationalist writers, even the liberal ones, nearly always stress the difficulty of obtaining consensus. Rousseau pointed the way in this respect as in so many others. He took it as axiomatic that man in society is so constituted that his own personal interests are generally opposed to his neighbor's:

> It will perhaps be said that society is so formed that every man gains by serving the rest. That would be all very well, if he did not gain still more by injuring them. There is no legitimate profit so great, that it cannot be greatly exceeded by what may be made illegitimately; we always gain more by hurting our neighbors than by doing good.[2]

Mazzini, the archetypal liberal-nationalist, illustrates the same pattern. He constantly preached against that "egoism" in human nature that divides class against class at the expense of the national common interest. Social cooperation, he argued, has to be induced by intensive civic education; social harmony is never achieved easily, much less automatically.

The most effective way to undermine faith in the necessity for the national State would be to show that social cooperation is now much easier to obtain than formerly and that in modern Western society consensus no longer requires the intensive cultivation which the institutions of the national State were designed to achieve. These arguments are commonplace in Europe today. What follows is an attempt to summarize the essential argument of a "good" European "federalist" who denies the relevance of nationalist theory to any new European political community.[3] It was economics, he argues, that made nationalism essential. In the eighteenth century liberal economics were cheerful, heartened by glowing expectations of abundance and automatic harmony. But after Malthus liberal economics became the gloomy science.

2. J. J. Rousseau, "A Discourse on the Origin of Inequality" in *The Social Contract and Discourses*, ed. G. D. H. Cole (New York, Dutton, 1950), p. 275.

3. This summary of opinions is based upon extensive interviews with officials and partisans of the Communities during the summer of 1963. For further sources, consult the Bibliographical Note. For my own attempt to analyze the basic assumptions of the federalist and nationalist approaches to European unity, see my recent book *Europe's Future: the Grand Alternatives* (New York, Horizon, 1965).

The actual economic situation in the nineteenth century supported the prevalent pessimism about human nature and society. The emerging industrial economy eluded almost every attempt by collective intelligence to bring it under rational control. Production had not yet reached the "take-off point,"[4] and there was real scarcity. Moreover, economists had not yet gained enough mastery over the workings of the market to prevent the extreme cyclical oscillations that so often led to scarcity and hardship when productive capacity was adequate but inefficiently organized. As a result, large portions of the population suffered economic hardship and insecurity and hence were susceptible to the blandishments of those who urged them to redress their economic weakness by seizing political power. To counter the quite understandable discontent of the lower classes required a continuous cultivation of national loyalties. Consensus remained a precarious accomplishment because it necessarily depended so heavily upon psychological rather than economic supports. It became essential to bring the common people into the government so that they might identify their interests with the nation's. No regime could maintain its precarious legitimacy without universal manhood suffrage and constant appeals to popular interest and loyalty.

In addition, the federalist's argument continues, the decline of Christianity served to bring the people into politics. It is a commonplace of cultural history that in that earnest but doubting age the spiritual energy normally intended for religion was increasingly diverted into politics. The State became the Church as well—a tendency noted by Coleridge. The individual was expected to find salvation as a citizen participating in democratic government. Manhood required suffrage. No longer was the average man content to leave government to professionals. He was constantly told it was his moral duty to have an opinion on the great issues of the day. His duty required all the apparatus of representative democracy and all the paraphernalia of the national State. In summary, during the nineteenth century powerful economic and cultural forces combined to make both popular

4. The notion of a "take-off point" and its implications are explored by W. W. Rostow, *The Stages of Economic Growth* (Cambridge, Cambridge University Press, 1961).

government and nationalism nearly inevitable. It was no accident that the partisans of the one were almost invariably the partisans of the other.

But in the years since World War II, our federalist continues, the fundamental economic and cultural situation has undergone a change so basic that it constitutes a profound revolution in human affairs. In Western states, the control of man over his economic environment has at last reached so advanced a stage that the old problems of scarcity and misallocation of resources can be set aside. The prevailing abundance will in turn eliminate the need for that intense cultivation of loyalties so essential to maintaining social peace in the nineteenth century. Economic scarcity and inefficiency no longer make the competition of classes an unavoidable evil. Politics is no longer dominated by a grim competitive struggle for scarce resources.

Moreover, politics has lost much of its spiritual baggage. Art and Sex are the new religions; the general public's enthusiasm for politics has waned. After so many wars, nationalism is discredited. Even communism has lost its evangelical fervor, at least in the Western World. Popular government has not created a race of supermen, led automatically to world peace, nor ennobled the dialogue of politics. It is more nearly in the category of a necessary evil than a panacea.

As a result of these changes the machinery of government can at last be extricated from mass politics. It is now possible for government to be run by dispassionate experts who rationally plan the growth of the economy, anticipate change, and eliminate its harmful effects on the displaced. Under this kind of regime no one need be deprived of his reasonable share of the general opulence. In such a world, where no one is hurt, the maintenance of consensus is not the desperately arduous task it was. The nation-state, with all its paraphernalia, is therefore obsolete. Where important decisions are made, the formal trappings of sovereignty and legitimacy are unnecessary. The European "plan" will emerge not from the inane slogans of mass political campaigns, but from intelligent bargaining managed by skillful experts. There is no need to make a State out of Europe in the traditional sense. The national State is obsolete because the economic and cultural conditions that made it necessary no longer exist.

I am tempted to say of this federalist argument what Coleridge said of Hobbes' theory of human nature: "Its statement is its confutation." Two familiar strains in Western political eschatology combine: faith in science and faith in experts. Nothing is done, of course, without faith in something. And perhaps we are really heading into a new age of fantastic commercial prosperity. Perhaps the gloomy predictions of the neo-Malthusians can safely be disregarded. There will be plenty of seaweed to eat and there will even be room to sit down, if not on earth, certainly on the moon. The rich nations will get richer and the poor nations will stop getting poorer. Bombs will be banned. Blacks will love whites. The lion will lie down with the lamb. All the world will be Sweden. Yet even in the midst of plenty, man gets bored. Human greed and competitiveness have seldom been incapable of surpassing the available supply of abundance. Coleridge touched the basic issue in his critique of the classical economists. He reckoned that economic scarcity in his day resulted not from a failure in productivity, but from excessive demands that arose from cultural rather than economic causes. Economics can never ignore ethics; opulence is not a cure for evil. There can never be automatic, enduring harmony in human affairs. Achievement results from intelligent effort and good luck. And what has once been gained must always be protected.

Coleridge's argument is as applicable today as it ever was. And since the basic problems of consensus in a political community are the same, his insights into the nature of the modern State should have more than casual relevance to the contemporary problems of nation-building. Coleridge, who was violently opposed to any wider European political association in his own day, might seem an unlikely source for ideas about a new European or Atlantic community. But such a judgment is superficial. For Coleridge European unity on the Napoleonic model would have meant the imposition of an alien despotism upon various free and self-sufficient peoples, the British included. He preferred his own national State, based upon consent rather than force.

Today, needless to say, the alternatives are different. Should

Britain eventually participate in the creation of a new European nation, it will presumably be because that seems the best way to preserve the health and growth of the society Coleridge loved so deeply. He knew that the national States of his day were not made forever in heaven, that they were the product of history. He was doubtless quite aware that Britain was not formed by the spontaneous fusion of England, Scotland, Wales, and Ireland. History had set the boundaries of nations; presumably history could change them. In short, in discussing the present relevance of Coleridge's type of nationalism it must be remembered that there is nothing that ties his definition of the State to any specific national context. What is essential to his definition is that the context must be limited, that a worthwhile consensus can only be achieved within a limited community of interests, loyalties, and identities—that such a community can never be universal.

We should not be misled because what would be in effect new national States are called "supranational." From the point of view of the ardent Scot London may be a supranational government. That does not keep Great Britain from being a "national" State. It may be useful to speak of a "federal" State in distinction to the tight centralization that seems an undesirable feature of some of the old States of Europe. But again, we should not be misled by terms. Federalism in this sense is only a particular form of constitutionalism, desirable because it seems the most effectively practical means to create a coherent political community which at the same time preserves the liberties and balances essential in any good State. In other words, federalism and Coleridge's kind of national State are not necessarily incompatible. The United States is both.

If the supranational State is not so different from the national, it will be surprising if the needs of supranational States bear no resemblance to those of nineteenth-century nations. Problems can differ in magnitude and remain similar in kind. This is not to say that the new European institutions should necessarily parallel those of national governments, let alone those of England in 1830. But whatever institutions evolve on behalf of the European Idea, some familiar difficulties will remain. Balances will still have to be created out of contentious diversity. There will still be rich and poor, radicals and conservatives, intellectuals and businessmen, north, south, east, and west. Unless we stand poised on the edge of the millennium, these interests can eventually be expected to clash in the usual ways. Some concept of the general interest of the whole must be invoked if the resulting issues are to be resolved by free men. Will the demands of Permanence and Progression be any less real? What of Active and Potential Power? The initial problem may be to give force to the active central power, but the ultimate health of the community will depend upon the creation of a potential power no less loyal to the community as a whole. Amid all the confusions of a State of many nations, the need for a Clerisy to articulate the vision of a larger commonwealth will be all the greater. Nor are the citizens of the new union likely to be as sophisticated as Milton and get along indefinitely without a personified symbol of general allegiance. People cannot be asked to make sacrifices for, or to love, things that are not real to their imaginations.

In short, unless the politics of the new Europe are to be based upon force or magic, the old problems of consensus will persist. Today is surely a time for creative thought, but not for theories that assume the world was created in 1945.

At the beginning of the last century, modern industrialism and the French Revolution presented a tremendous challenge to the political imagination of the Western world. The most humane and successful response was the constitutional nation-state. Today the challenge to creative political thought is hardly less demanding. Coleridge's writings furnish an impressive and sophisticated study of the modern national State. There is, moreover, an admirable spaciousness to his view of politics. His imagination held not only a soaring vision of the whole, but an intense awareness of those untidy details that determine what life is like for the average citizen. It would be surprising if his insights were irrelevant to what we possess at the moment or to what we would like to create in the future.

Bibliographical Note

My chief sources for Coleridge's political philosophy are *A Lay Sermon Addressed to the Higher and Middle Classes on the Existing Distresses and Discontents* (1817), *On the Constitution of Church and State According to the Idea of Each* (1st ed. 1830), and *The Friend: A Series of Essays to Aid in the Formation of Fixed Principles in Politics, Morals, and Religion* (1st ed. 1809–10). There is also the first "Lay Sermon" entitled *The Statesman's Manual: or the Bible the Best Guide to Political Skill and Foresight* (1816). In all cases, I have used the later revised versions of these works, edited by Henry Nelson Coleridge, as they appear in *The Complete Works of Samuel Taylor Coleridge*, ed. W. G. T. Shedd (7 vols. New York, Harper, 1858–68). In addition, I have made great use of the Coleridge Notebooks in the British Museum (Add. MSS 27901 and 47496–47550) and in the New York Public Library, Berg Collection. They are gradually being published as *The Notebooks of Samuel Taylor Coleridge*, ed. Kathleen Coburn (London, Routledge and Kegan Paul, 1957–).

Additional sources for his political opinions were Sara Coleridge, ed., *Essays on His Own Times* (3 vols. London, Pickering, 1850); *Collected Letters of Samuel Taylor Coleridge*, ed. Earl Leslie Griggs (4 vols. Oxford, Clarendon Press, 1956–59); *Memoranda suggested during a Perusal of the Minutes of Evidence before the Select Committee on the State of Children employed in Manufacture*, 1816, New York Public Library, Berg Collection, and "Table Talk," *Works*, 7. I have also used "Remarks on the Objections which have been urged against the Principle of Sir

Robert Peel's Bill" (1818), and "The Grounds of Sir Robert Peel's Bill Vindicated by S. T. Coleridge" (1818), reprinted along with a useful miscellany of Coleridge's political and philosophical writings in *Inquiring Spirit: A New Presentation of Coleridge from his Published and Unpublished Prose Writings*, ed. Kathleen Coburn (London, Routledge and Kegan Paul, 1951).

For Coleridge's general philosophy, in addition to *Church and State, The Friend,* and the Notebooks, I drew heavily upon the *Biographia Literaria,* ed. John Shawcross (2 vols. Oxford, Clarendon Press, 1907); and the material and the commentary presented in Kathleen Coburn, ed., *The Philosophical Lectures of Samuel Taylor Coleridge* (London, Pilot Press, 1949); Alice D. Snyder, ed., *Coleridge on Logic and Learning* (New Haven, Yale University Press, 1929); and *S. T. Coleridge's Treatise on Method* (London, Constable, 1934).

A sympathetic if difficult overall study of Coleridge's philosophy is John H. Muirhead, *Coleridge as Philosopher* (London, George Allen and Unwin, 1930). There are innumerable studies of Coleridge as poet and critic. Two that I have found provocative and helpful in this particular study are I. A. Richards, *Coleridge on Imagination* (Bloomington, Indiana University Press, 1960); and Basil Willey, *Coleridge on Imagination and Fancy,* Warton Lecture on English Poetry, British Academy, 1946 (London, Cumberlege, 1947). I have also made use of a recent study of Coleridge's religious thought: James D. Boulger, *Coleridge as Religious Thinker,* Yale Studies in English, 151 (New Haven, Yale University Press, 1961).

In recent years, two books have appeared dealing with particular aspects of Coleridge's politics. John Colmer, *Coleridge: Critic of Society* (Oxford, Clarendon Press, 1959), is an excellent study focusing upon Coleridge's career as a political journalist and upon his ideas about the particular social, constitutional, and international issues of the age. William F. Kennedy, *Humanist versus Economist: The Economic Thought of Samuel Taylor Coleridge,* University of California Publications in Economics 17 (Berkeley, University of California Press, 1958), notes the modernity of Coleridge's entire approach to economic problems and his important influence in the development of a modern tradition running counter to the Classical economists. Carl R. Woodring,

Politics in the Poetry of Coleridge (Madison, University of Wisconsin Press, 1961), discusses the political ideas in Coleridge's poetry. Two essays that deal with Coleridge's political theory are H. Beeley, "The Political Thought of Coleridge," in *Coleridge: Studies by Several Hands*, ed. Edmund Blunden and Earl Leslie Griggs (London, Constable, 1934): and John Stuart Mill's famous study, "Coleridge," *Dissertations and Discussions* (2 vols. London, 1859), vol. 1. General studies of political thought that discuss Coleridge at length are Crane Brinton, *The Political Ideas of the English Romantics* (London, Oxford University Press, Milford, 1926); and Alfred Cobban, *Edmund Burke and the Revolt against the Eighteenth Century: A Study of the Political and Social Thinking of Wordsworth, Coleridge, and Southey* (London, Allen and Unwin, 1929).

A collection of excerpts from Coleridge's political writings is R. J. White, *The Political Thought of Samuel Taylor Coleridge: A Selection* (London, Cape, 1938); and also, by the same author, *Political Tracts of Wordsworth, Coleridge and Shelley* (Cambridge, Cambridge University Press, 1953).

A bibliography of significant books dealing with the term "Romanticism" would fill a small volume. I mention only two since they have played an important role in forming my own ideas. They are Jacques Barzun, *Classic, Romantic, and Modern* (Garden City, Doubleday, 1961); and Arthur O. Lovejoy, *The Reason, the Understanding, and Time* (Baltimore, The Johns Hopkins Press, 1961).

There is an ever growing number of books on the subject of European integration. The functionalist approach with which I contrast Coleridge's nationalism is ably spelled out in such books as Uwe W. Kitzinger, *The Challenge of the Common Market* (Oxford, Blackwell, 1962); and Roy Pryce, *The Political Future of the European Community* (London, J. Marshbank in Association with the Federal Trust, 1962). A broad survey of the whole European movement is Henri Brugman's, *L'Idée Européenne, 1918–1965* (Bruges, De Tempel, 1965). I attempt to analyze the basic assumptions of the federalist and nationalist approaches to European unity in *Europe's Future: The Grand Alternatives* (New York, Horizon, 1965).

Index

155

Yale Studies
in Political Science